Praise for *Shortcut to Prosperity*

"Mark Hopkins' shortcuts are proven techniques to identify your strengths as you build your own competitive advantage. The book is written in a manner that is easy to read, comprehend, and *do*. It is a wonderful compilation, describing how inspiration and perspiration can work toward building success."

> —James Ellis, dean, Marshall School of Business, University of Southern California

"After finishing *Shortcut to Prosperity*, you'll do things differently—and better. Make time to read this book."

> —Jimmy Calano, cofounder and retired CEO, CareerTrack

"*Shortcut to Prosperity* is a wonderfully unique collection of real-world common sense and wisdom for entrepreneurs of all ages. This book should have been written long ago!"

> —Fulton Collins, chairman and CEO, Network Communications; vice chairman, International Board, Young Presidents' Organization

"In the words of Seneca, the Roman philosopher, 'luck is when preparation meets opportunity.' Mark Hopkins shows in a powerful and practical way how you can make your own luck, and be happier, healthier, and more successful as a result."

> —Robert Halperin, executive director, MIT Center for Collective Intelligence

"Mark Hopkins accomplishes a rare feat in *Shortcut to Prosperity*, meting out practical how-to wisdom right alongside earnest encouragement. Those looking to capitalize on their innate strengths and live a more energized life should read this book."

> —Aaron Kennedy, founder and former CEO, Noodles and Company

"I recommend this book to anyone at any point in their career trajectory. It is a wonderful tool for evaluating where you are, where you want to go, and how to get there."

> —Katherine Gold, president, Goldbug

"*Shortcut to Prosperity* provides young people clarity on the values to embrace and the habits to develop to excel in their careers and their personal lives. I highly recommended this book to my son and to anyone else who wishes to live a meaningful life."

> —Chris Crane, founder, president, and CEO, Edify

"For those unwilling to settle, *Shortcut to Prosperity* provides a game changing roadmap for personal and business success."
    —David Prokupek, chairman and CEO of Smashburger, voted #1
        most promising company by *Forbes* Magazine

"Mark Hopkins has captured the magic of great entrepreneurship and boiled it down in 10 practical 'shortcuts.' The power of his approach is masked by the clarity and simplicity with which he presents it. *Shortcut to Prosperity* is a masterful blueprint to a more effective and richer life. I wish I had read it as I launched my company!"
    —Zack Neumeyer, chairman, Sage Hospitality

"'How often is the status quo really what you want?' A challenging question from provocative author, Mark Hopkins. He presents a life-changing manifesto for navigating the path to prosperity. Whether you are early in your career or later in life, Mark's probing questions and insightful guidance will help you find your path."
    —Tom Joyce, executive vice president, Danaher Corporation

"Mark Hopkins clearly articulates core concepts I use every day that are the fundamental building blocks to a rich and rewarding life."
    —Tim Miller, CEO, Rally Software

"Mark reminds us how important it is to spend your time doing something you're passionate about, and how easy it can be to turn that passion into prosperity."
    —Mike Fries, president and CEO, Liberty Global

"*Shortcut to Prosperity* takes years of successful entrepreneurship experience and condenses it into a very easy-to-read format with great actionable steps. I recommend it to all my students and clients."
    —John M. Torrens, PhD, professor of entrepreneurship,
        Syracuse University

"Successful entrepreneurs aren't created by happenstance; they learn from others, look within, develop their raw potential, and create their own pathway to prosperity. Mark Hopkins shows the way."
    —Nathan Thompson, founder and CEO, Spectra Logic

"Entrepreneurs are different. We recognize that there isn't just the answer at the back of the textbook. We're all about finding the path of least resistance to help us grow our companies faster, easier, and more profitably. Mark's book will help give you a few more shortcuts to make this happen."
    —Cameron Herold, former COO, 1-800-GOT-JUNK; serial
        entrepreneur; and author of *Double Double*

SHORTCUT TO
PROSPERITY

10 ENTREPRENEURIAL HABITS
AND A ROADMAP FOR AN
EXCEPTIONAL CAREER

MARK HOPKINS

GREENLEAF
BOOK GROUP PRESS

Published by Greenleaf Book Group Press
Austin, Texas
www.gbgpress.com

Copyright ©2013 Mark Hopkins. All rights reserved.

Distributed by Greenleaf Book Group LLC

For ordering information or special discounts for bulk purchases, please contact Greenleaf Book Group LLC at PO Box 91869, Austin, TX 78709, 512.891.6100.

Design and composition by Greenleaf Book Group LLC
Cover design by Greenleaf Book Group LLC
iStockphoto of Maze graphic by SerJoe

Publisher's Cataloging-In-Publication Data
(Prepared by The Donohue Group, Inc.)
Hopkins, Mark (Mark John)
    Shortcut to prosperity : 10 entrepreneurial habits and a roadmap for an exceptional career / Mark Hopkins.—1st ed.
    p. : ill. ; cm.
    Issued also as an ebook.
    Includes bibliographical references.
    ISBN: 978-1-60832-430-9
    1. Entrepreneurship. 2. Success in business. 3. Financial security.
4. Career development. I. Title.
HB615 .H67 2013
658.4/21   2012950227

Part of the Tree Neutral® program, which offsets the number of trees consumed in the production and printing of this book by taking proactive steps, such as planting trees in direct proportion to the number of trees used: www.treeneutral.com

Printed in the United States of America on acid-free paper

13 14 15 16 17 18   10 9 8 7 6 5 4 3 2 1

First Edition

For Jennifer,
the love of my life and underwriter of my dreams.

Contents

DO SHORTCUTS REALLY EXIST?

The roar of the crowd matched the scream of the stock cars flying past the Talladega Superspeedway grandstand at almost two hundred miles per hour. On the last lap of the race, Penske Team driver Rusty Wallace was bumped from behind by racing legend Dale Earnhardt. A counterclockwise spin exposed the blunt rear end of the car to the massive airflow that had very recently been holding the car to the ground, vaulting the back of the car high into the air.

David Schenk was watching the action from his grandstand seat through the zoom lens of his Minolta 8000i SLR film camera, and he instinctually depressed the shutter when his brain alerted him that something was going terribly wrong on the track below. He captured twelve frames in quick succession as the race car seemed to float back to the ground, touching down with its front left bumper and launching into a series of end-over-end flips and twists that literally tore the car apart. Miraculously, Rusty Wallace walked away from the wreck with only a broken wrist.

David had the film developed and sent copies of the pictures to his brother and friends who had attended the race with him. One of the friends in turn sent a picture to the Roger Penske race team. A few days later, David got a call from a race team member who told him that the photo was incredible and they wanted to see any other pictures he had of the accident.

Back in 1993, NASCAR teams rarely got to see how critical parts of the vehicle performed in a crash, and David had captured the moment when the windshield popped out and another that showed Rusty's hand and wrist coming through the side window net. Both vehicle components were redesigned on the basis of what they learned from David's pictures.

This was the moment when David Schenk realized that his love of photography could possibly be more than a hobby. Buoyed by the experience, David contacted every publication that covered NASCAR in the hope of landing a part-time job as a race photographer. He got an offer from NASCAR *Winston Cup Scene* and spent the next two NASCAR seasons crammed into a hotel room on race weekends with ten other photographers who were following the series too.

Over two years, David had hundreds of his pictures published, and he evolved into the go-to photographer for *Winston Cup Scene*. His low-key approach and flattering candid shots helped David become the photographer preferred by Dale Earnhardt and other media-wary drivers.

Yet while all of this was happening, David still thought of photography as a part-time job to earn money while working toward his degree in chemical engineering. He increasingly found himself sitting through his lectures bored to death and wishing he were out with his camera instead. To his credit, David did finish his degree. In fact, he would probably be earning a living as an engineer today if not for a second intervention by an ally.

Tracy was a classmate whom David began dating his senior year. When she walked into his apartment for the first time and saw the beauty and power captured in the diversity of photos that decorated his walls, she immediately encouraged David to consider pursuing photography as a career—which he eventually did.

After initially accepting a scholarship to continue his studies in an MBA program, David changed his mind. He was increasingly aware of an internal tug-of-war being waged between the rational

David who thought he was supposed to become a chemical engineer and the creative David who wanted to pursue his photography. The day he made the gut-wrenching choice to follow his passion and give up his scholarship is the day he set himself on the path to true prosperity.

David leveraged his combination of creative skills (photography and graphic design) and technical skills (programming and computer) to become a website developer. Landing a job with Gibson Guitar, he became an accomplished studio photographer and webmaster, eventually earning responsibility for the online images for all fifteen Gibson divisions. High-profile clients like Peter Frampton came to appreciate David's creative vision and penchant for getting the perfect shot.

But he didn't stop there. David envisioned owning his own shop, where he would have the artistic freedom to choose the projects and people he worked with. Today, David and Tracy, now his wife, are partners in Schenk Photography, where they are simultaneously challenged and enthralled by their work. He smiles as he explains the stress involved in covering four simultaneous events in a single day—from green-screen fan photos at a Nashville Predators hockey game to a musician meet and greet at the Country Music Hall of Fame—and the offsetting and incredibly satisfied feeling he gets the next morning knowing that he figured out a way to make it all happen. As David tells his students in Junior Achievement, "What I do doesn't feel like work. Every day I get to do what I love, and that makes all the difference." Schenk Photography generates enough income for David, Tracy, and their daughter, Julia, to live in their lakeside dream home outside of Nashville. They work long but flexible hours, scheduling their work to accommodate the priorities of their young family.

Over the course of this book I will share inspiring stories of prosperous people, some of whom have made more money than David, but none who are better examples of prosperity—an existence that enables you to apply your passions, personal strengths, and values to work that is personally satisfying and fun while providing the financial resources to experience your envisioned life.

The world is full of people almost, but not quite, like David—smart, ambitious people who, in the quiet of their own minds, dream of hitting a grand slam home run in the game of life. The problem is the "in their own minds" part. Even though most of us want more out of life—more prosperity, whatever that looks like to you—we can't see the path to achieving it. Most people meander through life. For them, prosperity is happenstance, not a goal they've prepared for. They choose to ignore their internal compass when their compass says it is time to make a dramatic turn. Big change is hard and scary, especially when we haven't prepared for it.

And then there are the "lucky people," right? That's what we call them—"lucky bastards," if we're being honest. Some people, like David, seem to have a straight shot toward the exact life they want. We believe they were in the right place at the right time, or that they knew the right person, or that they had all the best advantages. Rarely are those things true. Yes, David had a few moments of luck along his path that led him to the right shortcuts—capturing the right shot at Talladega and meeting Tracy, his constant encourager—but he also refused to yield to the status quo and did the hard work required to earn a prosperous life. In fact, David's story epitomizes the three necessary components of true prosperity: thinking deeply about what we want, mapping the steps and leaps necessary to get there, and recruiting allies to help us along the way. Through trial and error, David discovered what prosperity meant to him and developed the skills required to make achieving his version of prosperity a likelihood rather than a long shot. I see these skills every day in the most prosperous entrepreneurs I know.

We are rarely taught these skills in school or at work, but they can absolutely be learned. And that is why I've written *Shortcut to Prosperity*. For most of my life, I've wanted nothing more than to understand exactly how to build the life I wanted. I'm an engineer, and I like to know how things work. Through the study of my own life and prosperous people from all walks of life, particularly entrepreneurs, I have identified the shortcuts I'll share with you in this book. Taken together, these shortcuts amount to the most fundamental shortcut: not having to learn the hard way.

Maybe you're early in your career and you aren't sure what your next move should be. Or maybe you are pursuing a path that has been erased by a new technology or business model. Or maybe you don't have a clear vision of what you want, but you know that you aren't satisfied or fulfilled by your current job, your income, even your relationships.

For you, for most of us, there is a more direct path—a series of shortcuts—you could be following to the life you want to lead. But just because shortcuts exist doesn't mean it's easy to spot them or take advantage of them.

Shortcuts Are Hard Work

Genius is 1 percent inspiration and 99 percent perspiration. So said Thomas Edison. Intuitively, most of us know this is true. We just wish it weren't. We hope that one day, in a stroke of luck, all of the prosperity we have hoped for will land in our laps. Frankly, that's why I titled this book *Shortcut to Prosperity*. I know that most people are looking for a shortcut. I'll let you in on a secret: Even shortcuts take a lot of effort and energy. Biz Stone, cofounder of Twitter, once quipped, "Timing, perseverance, and ten years of trying will eventually make you look like an overnight success."

Taking shortcuts doesn't mean doing things half-assed. In fact, sometimes the shortcut seems like the longer path. And taking shortcuts doesn't mean racing forward so fast that you can't have fun, can't stop and smell the roses. Sometimes, to be truly prosperous—which means enjoying life—we have to follow side routes when they seem compelling. You never know when or how new opportunities to experience your envisioned life will crop up.

The shortcut to prosperity is a mindset and practice of setting big goals, working smart, differentiating ourselves while finding synergies with others, and turning every win into motivation for the next step. The foundation of all of that hard work, all of those habits and behaviors, is one core principle: Add value in every interaction you have and to every opportunity that comes your way.

Consider this question: Who gets promoted in your company? In a well-led company it is usually the people who go all in, who make it their goal to find new and different ways for the company to succeed—and consequently for them as individuals to succeed. They add value every day. And that creative force requires energy. The first shortcut in this book is dedicated to generating the tremendous amount of energy you'll need.

Lack of energy and fear of wasted effort is what keeps most of us on a path that is less than fulfilling, exciting, or fun. It is the same path that has been followed by many others. Prosperity requires us to take a path that has not been trampled down by millions of other feet. Entrepreneurs understand this, sometimes intuitively. But it takes a lot more energy to peer into the future and determine our own course than to just stroll idly along, waiting for somebody to give us the next set of directions.

Yet this is what truly successful entrepreneurs do. For me, identifying opportunities to create value and then using these opportunities to differentiate oneself is the purest definition of entrepreneurship, whether the actual environment is a small start-up or a larger, more established organization. Being an entrepreneur is not necessarily about being a big idea guy. Nor does it require you to adopt the hit-and-run serial entrepreneur mentality. It means taking responsibility for one's future, and possibly the future of others, by filling one of the many voids created by an economy moving at the speed of light.

The Necessity of Personal Entrepreneurship

As I am writing this book, the global economy has been turned inside out by an information-powered revolution and an increasingly ubiquitous Internet that has, in many markets, annihilated the status quo and stalled the industry leaders that depended on it. Companies that haven't been able to adapt fast enough have failed or been acquired. The resultant restructuring has led to a high level of unemployment. In one of many side effects as traditional employers regroup, college graduates are finding it very difficult to get hired. In fact, according to the National Association of Colleges and Employers, in 2010 and 2011, only about 24 percent of graduating U.S. college students had a job upon graduation, and that was down from 26 percent in 2008 and 51 percent in 2007.

These events are just another upward spike on the chart of change in our world today. Because we tend to resist change, we struggle against it rather than letting it push us forward. We end up battered by it, tossed about in the torrent without a tree to cling to.

But if we learn the lessons of entrepreneurship, we can anchor our feet on the right path with our own strategic plans. We can depend on ourselves and carve our own paths. These are the serious measures you need to take to make yourself valuable—as all people with focus and an understanding of their own worth are. The future is brighter now than ever for the people who understand how the world works and can see where their passion intersects with the fast-changing environment around them.

In 2010, the Bureau of Labor Statistics released the results of a thirty-year study—National Longitudinal Survey of Youth 1979—that showed that the youngest of the baby boomer generation changed employers eleven times between the ages of eighteen and forty-four. What the release didn't indicate is whether those changes were voluntary or not. In either case the fact remains that recent generations of workers move about more often. So what is the end goal? Every time you move, make sure you are doing it strategically. Have a plan. Use the move to get you closer to your end goal.

If you are a "millennial," you may already be doing this. In a recent *New York Times* opinion piece entitled "Generation Sell" (November 12, 2011), William Deresiewicz, author of *A Jane Austen Education*, captured the power of entrepreneurship as an overriding social form. "When I hear from young people who want to get off the careerist treadmill and do something meaningful, they talk, most often, about opening a restaurant. Nonprofits are still hip, but students don't dream about joining one, they dream about starting one."

Even if you don't have that driving desire to start your own organization or business, personal entrepreneurship is still key to proving your value. Managers at failing companies are looking for people who can do what they are told. Managers at great companies know that their long-term success depends on recognizing and nurturing the few employees who are hardwired to identify, evaluate, and exploit new opportunities in the market by considering how the company can continue to add value. And if you can do this for your employer, you can certainly do it for yourself.

Whatever path you choose, it is always better to be the navigator. To do so, you must know *your own magnetic north*. For some, prosperity means doing something that no one has ever done before. For others, it means working for an organization that is changing the world for the better. For you, it might mean starting a company of your own. Our vision of prosperity also expands well beyond the work that we do. We have a vision for the whole life we want to lead. Family, friends, good deeds, travel. Passion. What we want is to experience passion in our lives and have the financial resources to follow whatever interests compel us to move forward.

Unfortunately, most people don't have any idea how to do this, where to start, or what kinds of talents or knowledge will help them achieve their goals. They keep walking in circles or heading east when their compass says west. They've abandoned their internal compass, and they have not learned the behaviors that will keep them on the right path if they stumble upon it. This book offers a method for reconnecting with your internal compass, a plan for finding the right path, and tools for developing the habits that will help you stay on that path.

But shifting direction isn't rocket science. It's just ten simple shortcuts.

How Ten Shortcuts Can Change Your Life

In gaming you get a lot of do-overs. In the game of life you get to play only once, and some choices you get to make only once. You can't afford the trial-and-error approach again and again. The purpose of *Shortcut to Prosperity* is to teach you how to make the most of your game—to share the skills, habits, and best practices that are not taught in school but are critical to achieving success in business and in life.

I spent the first fifteen years of my career in two Fortune 100 companies, and this experience taught me most of what I needed to know to be successful as an entrepreneur. And I was. Today, I help other entrepreneurs and organizations become successful. It took me most of my life to understand the shortcuts I'm writing about here, but once I did, they seemed obvious everywhere I turned. In fact, people just like you are doing amazing things in the business world and are enjoying the thrill of overcoming the challenges they set for themselves in life. I'll tell you their stories.

Part one of the book focuses on shortcuts designed to help you get started now and discover exactly where you want to go: What are you passionate about? What are your strengths and talents? What does your vision of the future look like? How does it compare to your current reality? Understanding how to launch the Prosperity Cycle and answer questions like these every day will keep you focused on a bright future and will ensure that you enjoy the trip.

In part two, I will show you how to create an unfair advantage over your peers by building a differentiating level of knowledge and expertise within an area that you are drawn to. How do you take the first step? How do you build on that foundation? And how do you not only spot but also assess those all-important opportunities in your path?

Pursuing prosperity is a team sport. In part three we'll tackle how to recruit allies to help you along the path, by genuinely caring about people, by aligning yourself with great partners, and by finding the best mentors.

Each of the shortcuts I'll explore in this book requires you to work for results. Developing the skills that will lead to your prosperity means working on the right things and committing yourself to a lot of practice. Contrary to popular belief, people aren't born with the abilities necessary to be great. They have to develop them. These behaviors can be life changing, and changing a life does not happen overnight. And yet, they are still shortcuts. Why? Because if you don't develop them as core skills, you may *never* get where you want to go. I'll help you build the right mindset, and I'll offer grounded advice for turning key behaviors into habits or skills.

The shortcuts in this book are designed to set you on a path of doing something different, something other people are not doing. This means that you have to train yourself to see opportunities that others don't, envision new models, develop the drive to make them real, and attract a whole lot of great people to help you do it. This is the road to prosperity in today's world. Everyone has the potential to see opportunities, but few of us recognize them when they are in front of us, and even fewer have the confidence to pursue them. Confidence comes from knowing that you are prepared and, perhaps more important, that you are not alone.

From a personal perspective, you need to discover your passions in order to develop a vision for your future, craft a road map that will keep you moving in the right direction, and surround yourself with people who will make the journey faster, better, and more fun.

Who needs a shortcut? You do. If you're ready to pay attention to your internal compass, it's time to discover the shortest path to your magnetic north.

Find Your
Field *of* "Play"

SHORTCUT 1: Power Up!

In 1977 Shannon Patrick Joseph Deegan was a gangly, tough, and athletically talented ten-year-old from Verdun, a working-class borough of Montreal. He played baseball and basketball well, but, as with most Canadian boys, his true passion was hockey. Even by Canadian standards he stood out as a talented center, having already traveled widely in Canada and even to the United States—which explains why he skipped school one winter's day and snuck into the Montreal Canadiens practice at the storied Montreal Forum ice rink.

Ken Dryden was in the prime of his career in 1977, already a hockey legend and playing for a Canadiens team that would win the Stanley Cup four years in a row (1976 through 1979). To this day, the 1977 team is widely considered to be the best hockey team in the history of the game.

So you can imagine the thrill that went through Shannon when Ken Dryden, about to take to the ice for practice, paused to talk to him. The world's best goalie took a long look at this tough young kid and asked him why he wasn't in school. While Shannon stumbled through an answer that he hoped had the best chance of keeping him out of trouble, Ken followed up with another question. He asked if Shannon was a good student, and Shannon told him, honestly, that he was. Naturally, the conversation then turned to hockey. Canada has a highly regimented youth hockey program that limits who plays where. In less than a minute it was clear to Ken that the kid was playing with the best teams that a ten-year-old could be invited to join.

Their two-minute conversation ended with an insight that set Shannon on a path that would change his life. Ken, who had played collegiate hockey at Cornell, told Shannon that, if he was a good hockey player and did well in school, he should pursue a scholarship in the United States. Now, Shannon came from a large Irish family, and neither his parents nor any of his seventeen aunts and uncles had gone to college. So, at the time, Shannon had no idea what a scholarship was. But that didn't change the impact of the moment.

Shannon's parents were in total agreement with Ken's advice and encouraged Shannon to focus on his academics along with his hockey. In 1983, after a lot of work on the ice and in the classroom, he was offered a scholarship to the University of Vermont. After turning eighteen his freshman year, Shannon entered the NHL draft and was selected by the LA Kings. Heeding the advice of Dryden and others who advised him to complete his degree, Shannon stayed in school, earning a bachelor of arts in psychology and political science while playing hockey. His last year in collegiate hockey was by far his best. His physical play, along with nineteen goals and twenty-one assists in twenty-nine games, earned him a two-year contract with the Kings—in fact, it was one of the most lucrative contracts offered to a collegiate player in 1987.

But then things started to get tough. His aggressive playing style and the resulting nagging injuries limited Shannon's play in his first year with the Kings organization. During training in his second year—the first year that Wayne Gretzky joined the club—he sustained another back injury that sent him to Finland to play in the less physical European league.

The injury didn't heal. A specialist eventually told Shannon that he needed surgery and that his hockey career was over, almost before it began.

For a lot of people, a hit like that would be the end of the story. They would give up on their dreams, believing that their one shot at fulfillment, excitement, and happiness was over, wasted. But not Shannon. Through his dogged pursuit of his hockey career, Shannon had developed an intuitive understanding of what it takes to realize prosperity in any endeavor: a self-sustaining cycle of motivation, effort, and achievement that fuels your internal fire, a fire that has to be grown from an initial spark. He didn't see his injury as the end, just the end of one iteration of that cycle. The next iteration was yet to come.

The toughest part of Shannon's journey was deciding early on that the status quo wasn't going to be good enough—and deciding to *do something* about it.

And that's what the first part of this book, and this chapter in particular, is about—making a start and then sustaining your energy. It is the hardest part of pursuing a personal vision of prosperity. For me, and for most people I know, taking the initiative to embark on any new path is tough. It may be hard, it may be risky, and where we are right now isn't so bad, really. Right? Maybe. But that first step may be the key to an amazing career and a fulfilling life. Most of us are prewired to further the status quo, but how often is the status quo exactly what we want? Rarely, would be my guess. But we cannot see the flaws with the status quo unless we are comparing it to a vision of something different, which requires us to think deeply about what it is that we desire.

Any project or opportunity or goal that you consider tackling is most intimidating the moment before you decide to make a start. The opportunity that you perceive, but have yet to pursue, can make you miserable. It hangs over your head, taunting you. Will you pursue it or won't you? What will happen if you do? What will happen if you don't? This uncertainty increases your stress level. The only way to feel relief is to give up on the opportunity entirely or to do something about it. The amazing thing is that any opportunity you actively decide to pursue, regardless of how big it seems, will become less intimidating the moment that you start to work on it. The whole point of this first shortcut is to convince you to find the inspiration for the first step and just get started. I'll show you how your initiative can become self-sustaining, even effortless, but only you can decide to make a start.

The Prosperity Cycle

Motivation equals success. Guaranteed. It might not mean immediate success. It might not mean success in everything you try. But strong motivation breeds inspired effort, and that will always lead to triumph eventually, even if it wasn't the triumph you were expecting. Most entrepreneurs I know can tell the story of how motivation to add value in a unique way led to a cool opportunity, even if it wasn't the opportunity they were initially hoping for.

Without a steadily burning fire that drives us to do the hard work and make the tough decisions to create the life we want, we won't be inspired to change. Passion, that internal fire, is the source of motivation. Without passion, you don't have much of a shot at prosperity, and this book won't do you any good. When you are living a life of prosperity, that passion is a roaring bonfire. When you aren't, it's smoldering ashes. Right now, you may not feel very passionate about any one thing in your life. Or you may have been persuaded that the thing you feel most passionate about isn't worth your energy, dampening the flames. You may not think of yourself as somebody who is inherently motivated. Many of us aren't. The Prosperity Cycle can help.

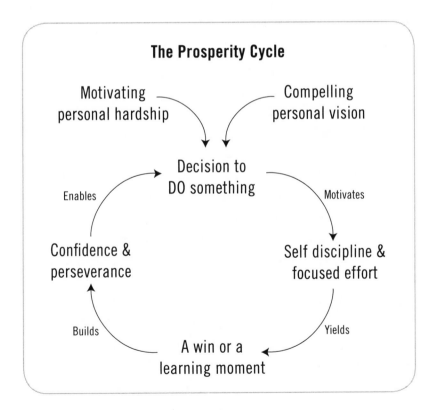

The Prosperity Cycle

Motivating personal hardship

Compelling personal vision

Decision to DO something

Enables

Motivates

Confidence & perseverance

Self discipline & focused effort

Builds

Yields

A win or a learning moment

The Prosperity Cycle offers a structured process for achiev-ing prosperity. It creates a perpetual feedback loop between your passions and your actions, propelling you forward down the path of your choice. Passion helps you get the cycle started, but the cycle itself reinforces your passion—powering your imagination and inspiring you to dream bigger and do bigger—"do" being the operative word. The Prosperity Cycle is a self-reinforcing cycle that will set you on your chosen path, keep you moving forward, and provide you with the vast amount of energy that you'll need to get where you want to go.

The most successful people, particularly entrepreneurs, use this cycle to their advantage every day, even if only intuitively. They are inspired by a hardship or a vision to step off the beaten track, where others are consistently telling them what is and is not possible. That first step, though, is prompted by a decision to do something, to embark on a new path toward a different goal. Whether your initial spark comes from being mad as hell or incredibly inspired, it's your ticket to ride. That energy and passion power the self-discipline required to get started and fuel the focused effort required to move forward. Effort always yields progress, even if it doesn't quite turn out the way you had envi-sioned. A win is fantastic, but a learning moment can sometimes be even more rewarding. Either can lead to increased confidence and self-esteem, which, in turn, motivate you to make the decision to do it again, only bigger.

Each success you rack up builds your capability and gives you the confidence to keep going bigger. More important, it fuels the perseverance referred to in Biz Stone's tongue-in-cheek com-ment about being an overnight success. There is no more satis-fying human experience than applying yourself to a problem, working hard to solve it, and finally knowing that you kicked its ass. Personal achievement is the human equivalent of nuclear fusion, releasing vast amounts of energy to tackle the next challenge in your path.

While this cycle is personal, let me be very clear that there is no way to sustain it without the help of others. Prosperity is not a solitary endeavor. We're talking about success, fulfillment, and happiness, and it's impossible to experience those things when you are alone.

The cycle of deciding to make a positive change followed by actually doing it, and doing it successfully, is habit forming—a healthy form of addiction. It's the addiction of the executive who grows a company at 70 percent a year. It's the addiction of the marathon runner or any high-performance athlete. You probably know someone like this, someone who always seems to be moving forward, who always has a goal in her sights and the plan and enthusiasm for getting there. You wonder where she gets the energy to do it.

It comes from the Prosperity Cycle. The cycle never ends for those who continue to fuel their internal fire, because even if they achieve their goals, life is full of new challenges and opportunities that renew the cycle.

Do Something!

The only prerequisite to experiencing the power generated by the Prosperity Cycle is the decision on your part to actually *do something*—to decide to invest the effort to take the first step toward what you want. I know you already have a complicated life, with more on your plate than you have time to accomplish, but so does everyone else. This is where you have the opportunity to separate yourself from the crowd and start to look different—like one of those people who are making things happen and making it look easy. But it's not easy, especially the first step, and most of us need a push. That push typically comes from one of two places: a personal hardship that has made you mad as hell and ready to fight, or a personal vision of the future so exciting that you would do anything to make progress toward it.

In the rest of this chapter, I'll look closely at what motivates us to start the Prosperity Cycle, while the rest of the book explores how to keep it going.

The Motivating Power of Hardship

Even at five feet two, Amber Freed is easy to spot in a crowd—she practically bounces down the street (always in a hurry), blonde hair flying and a full-face smile. You see, she has a great life. She's thirty years old and happily married, has a wonderful group of friends, and avidly volunteers her time and money for several charitable organizations. She is also no stranger to hard work, underwriting her lifestyle and philanthropy with a six-figure income earned as an analyst for an investment adviser in Denver. When we met, I couldn't help but be impressed. Amber is the real deal, a model of achievement. I was sure that she must have had a leg up in life and been taught how to be prosperous at an early age. I couldn't have been more wrong.

Born in Wyoming to a mom and dad who both have substance abuse issues, Amber had a life that was anything but easy. As a preschooler she lost everything but the clothes on her back when her dad burned down their trailer for the insurance money. They moved to a poor neighborhood in Montana. The house next door turned out to be inhabited by meth-cooking parents and their kids, who became Amber's playmates. The police shot the father during a raid, and the injured man took shelter on Amber's front porch. The image of the blood-stained concrete that they couldn't wash clean is etched in her mind to this day.

You would think it couldn't get worse than that, but you would be wrong. Her mom and dad's arguments over custody of Amber and her younger twin sisters led to moves from Wyoming to Montana to Texas to Colorado, back to Montana, and finally to Pueblo, Colorado. Along the way, Amber, not yet a teenager, got good at knowing when to hide the kitchen knives and how to make a 911 call that could end an out-of-control, drug-fueled episode without getting her parents sent to jail.

Sadly, the holidays were the worst. Extra time off from work just meant more time for multi-day binges that usually ended in her mom or dad's confinement to a treatment center at best or a suicide attempt at worst. One Thanksgiving, her dad got so angry that he grabbed the turkey from the oven and tossed it out the front door and onto the front yard. That set a precedent. In one-upmanship style, the turkey-in-the-front-yard gambit would be repeated at four more Thanksgiving celebrations.

I've never said, "I'm so sorry" so many times in an interview. But Amber was fine talking about it, wanting to share her story to help other young people, and wanting to explain to me how hardship powered her journey to prosperity.

And here's how it worked. Her family hardship was the source of motivation to begin a journey to a more prosperous life. During her gut-wrenching family experiences, Amber discovered that she had a choice—to be a passive accomplice to the caustic family environment surrounding her or to strike out in pursuit of a better life for herself and her sisters. She knew that breaking the cycle meant going to college but also knew that there would be no family money available to make it happen. No, the only way she would go to college was on a scholarship. "My only way to get out of Pueblo was to be the absolute best," she told me. "No room for failure, because I needed a full ride or I wasn't going anywhere."

Statistically, Amber was likely to follow her parents down the path of least resistance to a similarly self-destructive existence. But she didn't. Instead she focused her energies on being the best student she could be and experienced a reinforcing succession of academic successes that allowed her to build a reputation as an academic force in her small public high school. By her senior year, Amber had received a full scholarship offer to the University of Denver, where she would later earn a bachelor's degree in accounting and an MBA in five years.

Today, Amber looks back on her upbringing as a gift. How else could she have learned to be so resilient and open to change? She looks at the worst downside of challenges she has in her life today and they pale in comparison to what she's already overcome: "What's the worst that can happen to me? Lose my job? If everybody survived and nobody lost a limb, well, let's just laugh about it!" And when she recalls Thanksgiving turkeys on the lawn? "It's kind of hilarious. It's sort of awesome to have the turkey on the front lawn. Who does that?"

Hardship in life is a given. It's unfortunate, but we all face it. We lose jobs, we lose houses, we lose loved ones. We have tough childhoods. We have diseases. We can try to bury our struggles or let them defeat us, or we can use them to motivate us to a more prosperous life.

Daniel Coyle, in his book *The Talent Code*, calls motivating experiences, some harder than others, *primal cues*. It's a great descriptor. According to Coyle's research, no one is born with innate talent. Talent is developed through thousands of hours of "deep practice" powered by extreme motivation. But where does this motivation come from?

For our purposes, we can define a primal cue as a hardship that intrudes on a person's life. That hardship can provide a highly motivated response. Coyle's most fundamental—and tragic—example is the number of highly accomplished people who lost a parent at an early age. Members of this unfortunate club include Washington, Jefferson, Lincoln, Gandhi, Newton, Darwin, Michelangelo, Bach, Dostoyevsky, Keats, Twain, and dozens of others. The primal message that all of these high achievers received as a young person was, "You are not safe," translated as, "Holy crap. I'm on my own and I'd better make something happen here or I'm in trouble." Scary, but also highly motivating—a motivation that breeds paragons of personal entrepreneurship.

Since this is the last way any of us wants to be motivated, let's move on to a less traumatic example. Coyle noticed that his youngest daughter was a considerably faster runner than her older three siblings. He theorized that this might be the result of a primal cue: "You're behind—keep up!" When he researched his idea to see if he could find evidence to support it, he was amazed. In looking at the past ten world record holders in the 100-meter dash, he found that their average birth order was fourth in families of 4.6 children. Next he looked at the top ten all-time NFL running backs in yards per carry and found that their average birth order was 3.2 out of 4.4 kids. The message that these youngest siblings received—"Run faster!"—caused them to transform their average speed genetics into a world-class level of performance.

I considered the power of hardship to motivate as I thought about what makes some entrepreneurs so successful. Sometimes, when you're an entrepreneur, all you have is hardship: long hours, low income, an uncertain future, every day a roller coaster of triumphs and failures. Everybody knows the classic example of James Dyson's more than 5,000 failed vacuum cleaner prototypes. But the entrepreneurs who make it power through the down times and use them to learn, to inspire their next big move. More stories are out there than I can count of an entrepreneur who was almost down for the count, decided to give it one last push because of an idea that came out of the latest failure, and went on to become hugely successful. Rather than being deterred, these entrepreneurs have figured out how to use challenge as a foundation for the next right decision, to jumpstart the Prosperity Cycle.

Say you set a path toward a goal and partway down the road something happens that makes that goal nearly impossible. When that happens, you have to be resilient. You have to decide that the status quo isn't going to be good enough. You have to stay focused on how you will move forward.

If I put my own life under the microscope, I look back to age five to eight. During that period I attended four schools in three states. I developed few friendships and became horribly behind in school. If I had been in a different family I could easily have continued down that path, continued to do poorly in school, become isolated, and ended up leading a life very different from the one I was fortunate enough to lead. But I was part of an amazingly supportive family who helped me turn things around. We eventually settled down and I was enrolled in a good public school, was exposed to a healthy peer group, and was able to build on small successes and build momentum toward a happier life. You see, the Prosperity Cycle can begin at a very early age.

Is there or has there ever been a hardship in your life that could be a source of motivation to pursue a path to prosperity? I'm sure the answer is yes. While you may not have faced some serious motivating trauma early in life, like losing your parents, your hardships are your hardships and they are just as potentially motivating as anyone else's. Show me a person who doesn't perceive hardship in her life and I'll show you someone with a healthy supply of painkillers. Unless you are in denial, your life likely has some real aggravating stuff happening in it. Perhaps you have a boss who makes your life miserable and the situation irritates you to the point of making a job change or motivates you to the point of writing a business plan so you can become your own boss. Or maybe you are a middle child who never got the attention paid to the eldest or the baby of the family, and you use that to build a career as a performer. It doesn't matter what it is; if you perceive it as a hardship, you can use it to motivate yourself to start the change process.

Personal Vision—The Positive Motivator

Yes, hardship is motivating. There is no stronger innate force than our instinct for survival or self-preservation. But it isn't the only way we can be motivated to do something, to take action.

Many people develop a personal vision that is so exciting to them, so intensely motivating, that it sets them on a new path and gets the spark within them burning brighter. It leaves them no choice but to set a goal and adopt the discipline to make it a reality. I'm talking about a personal vision for what your life could be. Perhaps you get goose bumps from the thought of taking an idea for a new product and making it a gleaming reality. Or maybe you see yourself as a revered leader at your company. Or maybe you want desperately to travel the world or to have the resources to send your kids to great schools. For Shannon Deegan, the hockey player from the beginning of the chapter, it was to play in the NHL.

The amazing thing about personal vision is that it's a power we can *choose* to harness. While hardship and challenge are often acts of fate, the seeds of a personal vision already exist within each of us. The beginning of a personal vision is the personal compass that we can choose to pay attention to or not. So in shortcuts 2, 3, and 4, I'm going to walk you through the process of indulging your curiosity, diving deep to know yourself better, and using that information to develop a personal vision that gets your heart racing and your imagination soaring. Regardless of the source of your current motivators, if they are going to set you on a new path, they have to be strong enough to encourage change.

Choosing Prosperity

In a white paper on rethinking education, Seth Godin wrote, "The universal truth is beyond question—the only people who excel are those who have decided to do so. Great doctors or speakers or skiers or writers or musicians are great because somewhere along the way, they made the choice. Why have we completely denied the importance of this choice? Who will teach bravery?"[1] When I first envisioned the Prosperity Cycle, I entirely overlooked this crucial

---

1. Seth Godin, *Stop Stealing Dreams (What Is School For?)* (2012), available as a free e-book or audiobook at www.squidoo.com/seth.

fact. Prosperity requires a decision to be prosperous, and even when we have the motivators in place—positive or negative—some of us avoid making the decision. Geo Concepcion, whom you'll read about in shortcut 10, helped me realize it was missing.

The problem is that the decision typically requires choosing change. Change is hard, and most of us humans are prewired to hate it. But think about it in scientific terms. Change is the conversion of a source of energy—in this discussion, a motivator—into a new form of energy—the determination to make something new happen. That conversion is critically important in life; it is the act of fulfilling our passion. It's the act of actually living.

That point of decision, of choosing change, is the point that separates people who are prosperous from those who aren't. Most of us face it almost every day. Change requires getting off your butt and making a plan. It requires stepping off the path that you're on, because the path is miserable or because you can see another path that is more exciting. Either way, something brought the fire within you to life. It's now your responsibility to do something with it, but you'll accept the responsibility only if the motivation is strong enough.

Entrepreneurs understand this more than most because being an entrepreneur means being a change agent. It means doing something that hasn't been done before. Success and prosperity seek out people who are thinking out of the box and developing new capabilities in themselves as well as in the world around them. If you can train yourself to embrace change, you will differentiate yourself from the vast majority of people and dramatically increase the odds of achieving your vision of prosperity. As you become more comfortable with change, taking even just small steps to incorporate it into your life, each decision will become easier. And that is how the cycle self-perpetuates.

Once Powered Up, the Prosperity Cycle Never Stops

Shannon Deegan's personal vision was destroyed when he was told his professional hockey career was over. Was he disappointed to have lost his dream? Of course, he was absolutely crushed. But ten years of making his hockey dream come true had taught him that if he could come up with a new dream, he probably could figure out a way to make that happen, too. He understood the connection between effort and results. Instead of letting his feeling of loss paralyze him, Shannon used it to motivate the effort that he knew it would take to duplicate the success off the ice that he had achieved on it. A man who had become accustomed to taking big hits shook off the biggest hit of his life and was off in a new direction.

While Shannon was still with the Kings, a prominent Canadian politician had offered him a job after his hockey career was over, a time that they both thought was a decade or so in the future. Nine-and-a-half years ahead of schedule, Shannon made a decision, picked up the phone, and started his life after hockey. Shannon used the skills honed by hockey (hard work, preparation, street smarts, and communication) to excel in each of his career stops while learning successively more about what he liked doing.

Today, Shannon has his dream job: director of people operations with Google, a company people would almost kill to work for. It took many iterations of the Prosperity Cycle to get here, just as it did to get him to the Kings. Shannon can point to each of his previous jobs and explain how they prepared him for success at Google, but with a chuckle he'll admit that he didn't know where they were leading him at the time. He just kept making decisions that seemed right at that time, investing time and energy in the activities that he enjoyed and excelled at, and moving forward—working for more and more interesting companies in more and more demanding positions, going back to school to earn an MBA at Yale University, and eventually making his way to Google.

This is what a perpetual Prosperity Cycle looks like in real life. You get it started, hopefully when you're young, and then you keep it going, shaking off the disappointments while feeding off the succession of wins that continue to fuel your energy and efforts. Your path may be cut off at times and you'll have to find a new one, cutting through a lot of rough country to discover where you are supposed to be. This is when the Prosperity Cycle can be most helpful.

A lifetime of prosperity is going to take a lot of iterations of the Prosperity Cycle. You can't just jump into the middle of the cycle and hope for the best. Like achieving any really big objective, you start small, gaining the experience and confidence required to take the next step . . . and the next, and the next. Prosperity is a process with a beginning, a middle, and an end, which becomes the next beginning. All you have to do is choose to turn it into one.

Every time you decide to make a change and achieve a new goal, and then follow through with it, you are leveraging the Prosperity Cycle: to map a little more of your world, understand the power of self-discipline and effort a little better, use the returns on each personal investment, build your confidence, and trust yourself more. And then you're that much more prepared for the next iteration, however it begins and wherever it ends.

You can float aimlessly through life and have a small chance of stumbling on something that meets your definition of prosperity, or you can pursue it with energy and purpose. It's clear which one is the shortcut.

I thought of some of the best ideas for this book while riding on the cycling-friendly roads of Boulder, Colorado. That's what a lot of us do in Colorado—hit the road when the confines of the office constrict the flow of ideas and the only cure is a piercing blue sky and a bloodstream full of endorphins. After twenty or thirty minutes on my bike, whatever mental block I was struggling with is inevitably replaced by a new, exciting concept. That moment always ushers in a surge of energy that pushes me out of the saddle and makes me reach for a bigger gear.

I can't think of a better metaphor for what it takes to achieve prosperity—find something exciting enough to get you out of the saddle and reaching for a bigger gear. Figure out the first step in your own Prosperity Cycle and get going. Once you start, you'll never want to stop.

Finding the Shortcut

- You may not use it often, but you have already experienced the Prosperity Cycle in your own life. Think about an achievement that you had to work hard for and that you are proud of. Did it just happen? Of course not. You decided to do something, applied some self-discipline, and eventually made it happen. And it felt great. Go back to the Prosperity Cycle chart and trace through it with your achievement in mind. Use this example to internalize how the cycle works for you. Your path to prosperity is directed by how often you traverse this cycle. Prosperous people complete the cycle more often than less prosperous people. It's that simple.

- What is your motivation to enter the Prosperity Cycle? Are you currently mad as hell about something (hardship) and eager to overcome it? Or do you have a dream so compelling that you can't wait to begin to achieve it, cycle by cycle? If you know what it is, go to the shortcuttoprosperity.com website, print a copy of the cycle, and write it down at the top left (hardship) or right (compelling vision).

Do Something

- The very first step that you can take to launching your Prosperity Cycle is to decide to do the "Do Something" exercises here and at the end of every other chapter. Start now.

- The next three chapters will lead you through developing a personal vision, but it's never too early to start using the Prosperity Cycle. Identify something that you would like to make happen at work or at home. Make it something fairly simple. What is the very first step you need to make to achieve the goal? Make it granular, such as setting up a meeting or asking a colleague for help. Don't worry about the next steps for now, just take the very first step. Decide to make it happen and then just do it!

- One of the best ways to internalize the ideas in each of the shortcuts is to teach them to someone else. If you are serious about doing this, identify a confidant to discuss the concepts with as you learn them. Write that person's name down and make time to tell him or her about what you are doing to get the Prosperity Cycle started in your life.

SHORTCUT 2: Exploit Your Natural Curiosity

To say that Ernest Emerson makes knives is to say that Antonio Stradivari made violins. He makes the most coveted folding knives in the world. Navy SEALS won't go on a mission without one. NASA won't leave an astronaut on the space station without an Emerson knife. Customers routinely wait seven years for one of Ernest's custom blades.

Oddly, when I asked Ernest about his life in knives, he recalled a high school badminton tournament. In its heyday, this annual event in Ernest's small northern Wisconsin hometown attracted up to four hundred participants, many of whom came armed with expensive, custom racquets that Ernest couldn't begin to afford as a machinist's son. Ernest was curious to see how far he could advance in the tournament armed only with a cheap racquet from a backyard badminton set, a fitness level earned on the wrestling mat, and hand-eye coordination sharpened by years of competitive baseball. To give himself a psychological advantage, he gave the racquet a red and black paint job and dubbed it "The U.S.

Bomber." Ernest and his U.S. Bomber went on a run deep into the tournament, outhustling and exhausting opponents along the way. Far more important than his impressive third-place finish was what he learned about himself and the life lesson he took away from the experience.

Ernest realized that day (although it might have been obvious to an observer before then) that he enjoyed the thrill of competing solo, of wondering how far he could go with no one to blame but himself if the outcome wasn't what he wanted it to be. That drive, that curiosity, led him to become fascinated with martial arts, and in college, he joined the University of Wisconsin karate team. After graduation, while others were gravitating toward traditional career-track jobs, he indulged his curiosity and moved to Southern California to train at the Filipino Kali Academy, an institution devoted to teaching Jeet Kune Do, the fighting style created by Bruce Lee. He took a job at Hughes Aircraft as a machinist to pay the bills.

Part of Ernest's training required the use of a balisong knife, but he couldn't afford to buy one. Instead he drew on his day job and made his own knife, tempering the blade with a propane torch at his kitchen table. His workmanship was so good that other students asked him to make knives for them.

Thus was born Emerson Knives.

After becoming a martial arts instructor, Ernest followed his curiosity into a product development phase, exploring what it takes to create the best folding knife in the world. He imagined a knife that is dependable, durable, easily sharpened, corrosion resistant, and easily disassembled for cleaning and repair. Eventually a couple of "underwater welders," the label that low-profile

Navy SEALS sometimes give themselves, showed up at a knife show and explained why they loved Ernest's work and what additional needs they had for a knife. Emerson designed a knife called the CQC-6 (CQC standing for close quarters combat) that became a special forces icon and the first of many highly sought-after models designed for different purposes.

Has becoming a leading knife producer made Ernest rich? Yes. Could it make him much richer? Absolutely. But by his own estimates, he is able to supply only 30 percent of the demand for his knives, and to produce more would require a mass production process that is anathema to him. It would also leave less time for him to invest in the other opportunities he finds to follow his passions, like building ultra-high-quality electric guitars and muzzle-loading Kentucky rifles and learning to speak Russian.

If prosperity was only about the money for Ernest, he would do things very differently. Prosperity for Ernest means respecting the natural curiosity that has already brought him so much success and continuing to indulge the passions that result from that curiosity. It means pursuing projects so personally compelling that he routinely heads back out to his workshop after dinner because he would rather be there than anywhere else in the world.

If we do not acknowledge and pursue the questions that leap into our heads or the ideas we might like to test, we abandon opportunities to discover our true passions. And once we have found our passion, if we do not nurture our curiosity for it, we miss out on the opportunity to differentiate ourselves.

If we do not indulge our curiosity, it is almost impossible to achieve prosperity.

From Curious to Passionate to Prosperous

Entrepreneurs exploit the opportunities that most others don't see, using solutions that leverage insight that others don't have. Where does the superior insight come from? Hours upon hours of delving into the minutiae that determine the effectiveness of a solution. Good solutions are well thought out by people with a tremendous amount of relevant experience in a particular arena. How do you develop this level of knowledge? By indulging your curiosity, growing that curiosity into a defined and focused passion, and then letting that passion drive you to new levels of knowledge, ability, and understanding. This process is key to the Prosperity Cycle—because it makes it fun!

Superior insight and relevant skills are fundamental to seeing better ways to do things. And "better ways" are the heart, soul, and value of not only entrepreneurs, but of anybody who wants to develop a career and personal prosperity. You might think about it this way: A truly valuable player in a company brings two things to the table—strong ideas for continuous improvement and strategies for executing those ideas. These are the requirements of adding value. This is difficult to offer up if you aren't engaging your natural curiosity and wondering, "How could we do this better?" Can you do this outside of your areas of interest? Of course you can—it just takes a lot more effort.

If you are not enjoying yourself or simply are not very interested in what you are doing, the self-discipline and focused effort required to keep the Prosperity Cycle going once you've started it are vastly more grueling, and you are more likely to abandon it. Passion is the source of the draw of a compelling personal vision. Yes, you have to want the outcome, but if you are in no way excited about what it will take to get there, if you aren't curious about what you will learn along the way, you will easily be distracted and pulled down a different path. You may be able to earn a good living operating in an arena that you aren't passionate about, but it will be a slog and you will not achieve the version of prosperity that this book is about. True prosperity happens when you exploit your natural curiosity to fuel the many trips around the Prosperity Cycle that it takes to gain the insight and skill required to differentiate yourself from your peers.

The great thing is that we are all born with an innate sense of curiosity. All you have to do is observe a toddler. Every utterance is either an exclamation or a question. Most parents find it exhausting, but from the kid's perspective it is incredibly valuable. *How else am I to figure out how my world works?*

Some people seem to maintain that curiosity and develop a great sense of what they are passionate about. Jeff Bezos, CEO of Amazon, once said, "One of the huge mistakes people make is that they try to force an interest on themselves. You don't choose your passions, your passions choose you." Yet most of us struggle to define our passions. Our particular interests evolve from the interaction of our personalities and the world we have been exposed to. Sadly, throughout our lives, we're often discouraged from indulging our curiosity in those interests, though. Through our experiences growing up and in the working world, we're told that it doesn't always pay to question the status quo, that we shouldn't ask too many questions, that we should follow the rules. Or we're told that our passions are unrealistic and that we can't make a living by pursuing them. Or maybe they aren't appropriate because we are breaking tradition. The ways in which people are discouraged from doing what would really make them happy are almost infinite.

And yet, some people still manage to do it. Now, maybe they

were discouraged less than others. But I think it's more about learning to trust your internal compass and building confidence, recurring themes throughout this book. Prosperous people have trusted their instincts and pursued their interests, sometimes initially as a hobby and eventually as a vocation. If you feel far removed from your passions, it is time to rediscover them. Shortcuts 3 through 7 will help you reconnect with them and develop a plan that will help you build the confidence you need to pursue them.

Curiosity motivates the hard work of innovation. When you are following your curiosity and exploring an idea or discipline that you are passionate about, it's not work. It becomes effortless. You find yourself pushing past frontiers, until one day you are so deep that there's nobody else to turn to for answers. When that happens, you know that you've successfully pursued your passion—and had fun doing it. Along the way, you will have advanced through the Prosperity Cycle. Not only will your life's work bring pleasure and meaning, it will also bring a financial return if you want it to.

The first step is to discover what you are really interested in, what kindles that internal fire. There's no handy personality assessment out there to help. You have to trust your natural curiosity to guide you onto paths that will lead you to where you really want to go.

Indulging Your Curiosity Means Being a Lifelong Learner

The most successful people I know are *still* trying to figure out how their world works, whether their world involves engines, computers, advertising, or medicine. This is why I believe curiosity is one of the most potent shortcuts to prosperity. Every person that I interviewed for this book has it.

Most of us, especially students and young professionals, are learning what other people already know. This is where we all have to start (and I encourage it in shortcut 5, Learn from the Best). But the people who follow their interests have an opportunity to learn what few others know. They gain the ability to do things differently (and better!) than anyone else has ever done them. They add value. Their cutting-edge learning brings benefits to society, to the company they work for, and yes, to themselves. This is what anyone who is making the big bucks (legally!) is doing.

Jack Dorsey was nuts about maps as a kid. He couldn't get enough of them. But static maps weren't enough. He wanted to see what was happening on those pictured streets. So he bought a scanner and built software that would allow him to map the movement of ambulances and police cars. He soon realized that he was just showing what *had happened*, when what he really wanted to know was what *was happening*. Using these ideas, he landed a job developing real-time emergency dispatch software. But Jack's real passion was for real-time data, and so he was dissatisfied with his software "maps" of the city. They didn't have any people in them—the generators of real-time data.

And that is when Jack Dorsey began working on the prototype that would eventually evolve into Twitter. The cofounder of Twitter told this story in a talk at Stanford University titled "The Power of Curiosity and Inspiration."[2]

How does a person become this curious? How do they develop the drive to keep learning? In her book *Mindset*, Stanford

2. Jack Dorsey, "The Power of Curiosity and Inspiration," Technology Ventures Program, Entrepreneurial Thought Leaders Lecture, Stanford University, February 9, 2011.

University professor Carol Dweck identifies two primary mindsets that exist in every one of us: fixed or growth. People with a fixed mindset believe that their talents and abilities are set in stone—you either have them or you don't. Since they believe that everyone's abilities are predetermined, they spend their time trying to prove that they were born smart and talented.

One of the debilitating characteristics of the fixed mindset is that there is no upside to tackling a new, tough challenge. If you succeed, you've just proven what you already believed anyway. It's not exciting, and it doesn't necessarily help you become more confident. And if you believe you are innately intelligent, when you fail, it destroys your confidence. You struggle to rebound. With this mindset, it's better not to try anything too hard or risky in the first place. Dweck's research shows that parents and educators unwittingly reinforce this model by celebrating intelligence over effort. You are taught that you are either smart or not, capable or not, destined to succeed or not.

On the other hand, kids who are rewarded for effort instead of intelligence develop a *growth*, or learning, mindset. They don't get hung up on outcome and they become better learners. They view successes and failures equally as opportunities for growth, which they are. They are willing to take risks because they are less afraid of failure. And those risks sometimes lead to great rewards.

People lucky enough to have adopted a growth mindset early on know that their abilities can be (and are!) grown over time. In other words, their intelligence, character, and talents are not fixed, but grow in direct proportion to the experiences they have, the knowledge they acquire, and the effort they expend. And the best part is, even if you have a fixed mindset, it is possible to change it—as it is possible to change almost anything else.

You do not need to be a genius to get on the path to prosperity, because intelligence can be grown and talent can be developed. Dweck's research has shown that an IQ test is a measure of how much you have learned at the time you take the test. No more, no less. When psychologists Martin Seligman and Angela Duckworth studied 164 eighth graders looking for the contributing factors to a high grade point average, they found that self-discipline was twice as accurate a predictor of grade point average than a student's IQ. In *The Talent Code*, Daniel Coyle cites this study when discussing the development of self-discipline as a key factor contributing to the success that KIPP Charter High Schools have in driving up academic performance in their students. Self-discipline is a point on the Prosperity Cycle for good reason.

Remember Amber from shortcut 1? Her life wasn't easy growing up, and that could have set her on the path to a fixed mindset. But she was focused on achieving her own vision of prosperity. As she studied harder and harder to do well in high school, the learning process became second nature to her, and instead of just answering the questions in her textbooks, she started asking questions in fields that ran the gamut from nuclear power to the work of the Centers for Disease Control.

After she earned her BA and an MBA in just five years, her curiosity pointed her to a job with a big-four accounting firm, one of whose biggest clients was restating its financial statements because of accounting irregularities. Learning about what constituted fraud in a Fortune 100 company was interesting, but, in the end, it was still accounting. After two years she left to join a company that was planning an initial public offering, because she was curious about how that process worked. And after the IPO was completed, she left to become an associate equity analyst for a Denver investment adviser. In what she now considers the ideal job, Amber leverages her natural curiosity to ferret out all there is to know about a target company's financials, business model, key executives, ethics, and just about any other detail relevant to a proposed investment. Her efforts yield the type of information that drives the investment decisions that, in turn, contribute to the company's impressive track record of success.

If you are introduced to Amber, get ready to be peppered with questions. "I don't mean to do it, but I kind of grill people when I meet them. Where are you from? What do you do? Oh, yeah? What do you think of this company's strategy?" There always seems to be a question mark hanging in a thought bubble over her head, and she rarely denies herself the pleasure of getting the answer.

Yet Amber doesn't see herself as highly intelligent. In fact, she told me she sees herself as sort of a ditz and shared a couple of stories to back it up. Once, she took her car in for service and was confused when the receptionist at the dealership couldn't find her in the list of scheduled appointments—until she realized that she'd taken her Lexus to an Audi dealership. Another time, she locked herself out on the deck of her fourth-floor apartment. Her husband was out of town and her cell phone battery was dead. After trying, unsuccessfully, to break the sliding glass door window, she was able to get the attention of some passersby and convinced them to call 911. In a horribly embarrassing ending to the story, the fire department had to rescue her with a massive bucket truck that could reach the fourth floor.

What Amber does have (other than a great sense of humor) is an outsized curiosity and the equally outsized learning capacity that is naturally developed by curious people. She often finds herself in meetings where "scary smart" fund managers are talking way too fast about subjects that she is unfamiliar with and ends up with assignments that she has no idea how to accomplish. She laughs at times like this, telling her bosses that even though she currently has no idea what they're talking about, "I'll come back in two hours and appear very smart." Why? Because she is confident that because of the years of study in her chosen profession (finance) and her well-developed ability to learn, two hours is all she'll need to figure it out. A person with a fixed mindset would have run from the room screaming. Amber's growth mindset causes her to embrace challenge.

People who indulge their natural curiosity and program themselves to learn leave nonlearners behind over time, regardless of where they start. Opportunities for new experiences and learning surround all of us, all of the time. Curious people notice these opportunities and, because of their need to know more, pursue them. People who have lost the natural curiosity that they are born with don't see new opportunities, don't pursue them, and unwittingly undermine their ability to follow a path that offers fulfillment and other rewards.

Move Toward a Growth Mindset

If you have not already, ask yourself whether you believe you have a fixed or a growth mentality. What evidence do you have to support your conclusion? If you find yourself operating in a fixed mentality, the best and easiest way to move toward a growth mentality is to identify your natural passion and then start taking small steps to follow where it leads. To one extent or another, every person I interviewed for this book had a story about following their curiosity that led first to a development of competence and then to a growth mentality, and then later to a value-adding career yielding high levels of personal satisfaction and income—in other words, prosperity.

Following are some tools to help you develop or further a growth mindset and indulge your curiosity.

Appreciate Every Learning Opportunity

The obstacle that we face in moving toward a growth mentality is our fear of failure. Sometimes that fear is obvious to us, and sometimes it is not. Sometimes we don't realize when it is controlling us. Often, our fear of the repercussions of failure far outstrips the reality of what will happen if we fail. And because of the depth of the fear, we can't see all of the positive outcomes that can result from failure.

We've all heard the old adage, "You learn more from failure than you do success." According to recent brain studies, that may or may not be true. It depends on how we treat the failure. If we avoid thinking about it, if we let it affect our mental state or self-image, we actually may learn less from it than we do from successes because our brains respond to the chemical response of the positive experiences and change neural pathways accordingly. This may be particularly true of people with a fixed mindset. Each time that happens, a great opportunity to move forward on the Prosperity Cycle is lost. So here is an exercise that will help you gradually shift your approach and attitude about failures.

Once a week, look back and identify one or two key successes and key failures. They may be small or they may be big. Try to focus on wins and losses that resulted from trying something new, stretching yourself. For each, analyze what happened and consider what you learned from the experience. When you consider the failures, also think about how the result differed from what you thought it might have been. Over time, this positive-oriented analysis will help you change your attitude about failures, will help you see the silver lining, will help you appreciate opportunities for developing skills, talents, and intelligence and move you closer to a growth mindset. To learn more techniques, consider reading Carol Dweck's book or articles or books by Martin Seligman.

Ask Why Five Times

By giving your natural curiosity free rein, you are exercising your brain and continually building knowledge and understanding. The more of it you have, the faster each iteration of the Prosperity Cycle will be.

Early in my career I was fortunate to work for two companies (HP and Emerson Electric) that cared deeply about product quality. Many aspects of their quality approaches were based on the teachings of Dr. W. Edwards Deming, the guru of quality throughout the world. As I think back on Deming's teachings, I now realize that his tools work well because they are designed to leverage and amplify natural curiosity and the drive to solve problems. One of his simplest tools? Ask why five times.

Here's how it works. Have you ever gotten a shipment in the mail that was missing a critical piece? It's happened to all of us, and it is frustrating as hell. When we analyzed that problem at Emerson Electric, we went to the source of the problem (the shipping department) and asked why the heck they had shipped the box without a key part. The answer was "We're really busy back here and sometimes we don't get everything into the box." An unenlightened supervisor without the curiosity to investigate further might simply fire that employee. The problem was, we had already done that—many times—and the shipping errors continued. Here's what we learned when we asked why five times (the first why being the question above).

- Why is it tough to get the right parts in the box? Answer: There are a lot of different parts that need to go in the box and it's hard to tell if you have them all there when you seal it.
- Why is it hard to tell if the right parts are in the box? Answer: Because the packaging doesn't allow you to see if everything is there.
- Why isn't the packaging designed so that you can tell at a glance if everything is there? Answer (from packaging designer): We thought it was too expensive to design pockets for every part so that the parts could be verified at a glance.
- Why did you think it was too expensive? Answer (from the customer service manager): Because we never explained to the packaging designer how expensive and damaging to our reputation it is to take calls from angry customers and have to reship orders at our cost.

Solution: Redesign the product packaging to make it easy to get the right stuff in the box. By asking why five times, we used a process that any curious ten-year-old could follow to get to the root of the problem that had hurt our customer service for years.

Our natural tendency to ask why is often suppressed when we get answers like "Because that's just the way it is" or when we're told, "Just accept it and move on." It's hard to overcome those environmental influences, but if you want to discover your passions and achieve prosperity, you'll find a way. There are better ways to do everything, and if you trip over a big enough one, it just might be the insight that forms the foundation of your next company, your next career move, your next revelation. So every time you are wondering how something works, you should take the time to think about why it works that way. Put your mind to work thinking about why something may be the way it is and see if you can imagine something better.

Other Ways to Indulge Your Curiosity

If an Answer Doesn't Seem Right, Don't Accept It:

Possibly the most commonly heard excuse in the middle of a crisis is, "That's what I was told." It is a cop-out, a crutch of the unmotivated and incurious. When you find yourself accepting answers that you believe are wrong, it is time to change your environment, because you are no longer curious at all about what you are doing, or you're fearful enough to let your environment suppress your curiosity. The passionate don't accept wrong answers. They dig for the right ones.

Find Your Own Solution:

In shortcut 5, I'll encourage you to learn from the best to accelerate your learning process. However, indulging your curiosity sometimes means finding your own answers to questions. The next time you discover a problem, rather than assuming that somebody else will solve it or asking somebody to solve it, find your own solution. Do the legwork, go down the rabbit hole, and create a solution that you think will work.

Look for Connections:

Some of the most powerful insights, which can become the source of passion and energy, occur when we make a connection between two things that don't seem to be related. Look for connections between your world and new information or ideas that you discover. Take the time to ponder them. Some of the most powerful innovations come from taking knowledge that is commonplace in one setting and using it to solve a problem in a completely different space. My background in contract manufacturing, for example, taught me to constantly look for systemic ways to get the right product to the right customer at the right time. To this day, I can't walk into a consumer-oriented shop (restaurant, rental car agency, coffee shop) without seeing multiple examples of process changes that would improve their customer experience.

Life Is a Trip Down the River

Think of our passage through life as a ride down a meandering river. We all start with the basic means to stay afloat, a simple raft of sorts, and we begin our passage on the river watching the world go by. Not a bad way to go along, really. The world floats ambiguously by us and we don't have to think about much as the current carries us. Some people scarcely take notice of the details or meaning of the scenes that are streaming past. But others start to realize that the activity passing them by looks interesting—people doing things they don't understand and having fun doing it. The most curious of the adventurers begin to think of ways to steer their raft so that they can explore what interests them. Pretty soon they're fishing driftwood out of the river and fashioning rudders and paddles. Maybe they lash their raft to others and combine resources to make bigger rafts capable of negotiating any part of the river they choose to explore. What we end up with is a whole range of people and crafts, with some of us sitting on the raft we started with and others buzzing around in watercraft that look like America's Cup yachts.

You can't start exploring your world without the curiosity to care where you are going in the first place. And the trick to rediscovering your natural curiosity (if you ever lost it) is to adopt the growth mindset—the mindset that tells you that challenges are learning opportunities and that there is no such thing as looking dumb. There are only chances to get smarter.

In the next shortcut, we'll explore how to go even deeper in your self-exploration to better understand the values and talents you possess so that you can leverage everything you've got to develop a powerful, motivating vision for your future success.

Finding the Shortcut

- Do you have a fixed or a growth mindset? Many of us have an internal voice that leans toward a negative or fixed mentality, focusing on why you can't do something. Banish it with the following mantra: I can learn anything that I want to commit the time and effort to understand, and the more I learn, the more prosperous I'll be.

- Change is easier when you are surrounded by people who model the behavior you are trying to achieve. Make a list of the most curious, dynamic, successful, and fun people you know and find ways to spend more time with them.

- What mindset does your teacher, boss, or mentor have? If it's not a growth mindset, you will be well served by replacing that influencer as soon as you can.

Do Something

- Choose a subject that you are curious about and spend a month learning about it. By all means, scour the Internet and put a good book on your nightstand, but also find a living, breathing person who is an expert on the subject and will agree to be interviewed over coffee or lunch. Don't worry, experts love talking about their expertise, and the majority of people are willing to take the time to guide someone with a genuine interest. The dynamic nature of interacting with a person will deepen the learning immensely. Look for a niche within the subject that you are especially interested in and follow up. It may just be the nexus of your next career.

- Consider two problems you face at work and complete the following statement a few times for each problem: "Things would work so much better if . . ." What did you come up with? Rank these solutions in order of how curious you are about them—about how they might work, about how they could be implemented. Make a plan to address the one you are most interested in and ask your boss for permission to experiment with it. You will be learning and differentiating yourself from your peers at the same time.

- Set a recurring appointment on your calendar, blocking out time each week to research or think about a problem or opportunity you encountered. Do it now! Google makes it a practice for their employees (they're expected to spend 20 percent of their time being creative and working on personal projects unrelated to their standard work), and look at where it's gotten them.

SHORTCUT 3: Nosce Te Ipsum—Know Thyself

When Mike Aviles talks about the document that has helped shape his life for the last eighteen years, he does it in a steady cadence colored by a subtle Brooklyn brogue. It all started, he explains, when he hit a wall in his career. In 1994, Mike was four years out of Stanford Business School, married with two very young children, and thirty-four years old. He had spent the previous four years helping to build a company from $65 million to $450 million, and he wanted to be CEO. So he was very happy when the current CEO said to him, "You can run this business someday."

"Great," Mike said. And then he thought to ask, "When's that gonna be?"

"Well, I'm thinking about retiring early—when I'm fifty-five," the CEO said.

He was forty-two at the time.

I'm not waiting thirteen years, thought Mike. And so he started to plan his next move. "I wanted to be CEO. I wanted to be on the cover of *Fortune* magazine. I wanted these claims to fame based on what I would do in the business community. And I was going to drag my wife and my kids along with me. And boy, were they going to be proud of me," he said, with building sarcasm. "If you would have asked me then, I would have said that success in my career would be at the top of my list of goals."

A believer in personal growth methodologies, Mike decided to sit down and make a list of goals before making any big moves. He asked his wife to do the same, wanting to make sure that they were on the same page. He worked on his list over a period of days, narrowing it down until he had whittled it to five. Then he began the task of prioritizing. When he was done, this is what he had on a sheet of paper:

1. Maintain health, hope, and happiness in the Avileses' lives.
2. Have financial and personal flexibility.
3. Continue personal development.
4. Be a respected leader in the community.
5. Realize my professional potential.

Of the five life goals, only one was professional. And instead of his career being first, it was last. In fact, he discovered, it was really just a means for achieving the first four things. "What I came to realize is that if I didn't achieve those first four things, even if I became another Jack Welch, I wouldn't be happy. But the other way around? If I had achieved those and not the heights of professional success? I would be perfectly happy."

Knowing something and acting on it are two different things, though. Changing our behavior isn't easy. Despite his list, Mike knew he was not a "balance" guy. He could always justify why he had to work late or on a Saturday. His wife never complained and his kids were too young to. But four years after making his list, after he had moved to another company to be CEO and that company was sold, he took his foot off the pedal and looked around to see what he was missing. It was his family. *My kids are growing up without me*, he thought. *Whatever I do next, I need to be able to balance better.*

And so he used his awareness of his values and his weakness in finding balance to design his next CEO gig. It was a mile from his house and three miles from his kids' school. At 6:15, even if he was in a meeting, he would say, "I've gotta go. I'll be back in forty-five minutes." And he would go home to have dinner with his family. Family and kid events got first billing on his calendar, and everything else would be slotted in around them. "I still worked like an animal, but I would find ways to do it all because I wanted to do it all."

This decision, and many others over the past eighteen years, has been guided by what started as his one-page list of goals and evolved into an expansive document that he calls "I Am." In it, he has analyzed his inspirations, his strengths, his weaknesses and fears, what he wants, what brings him life, what drags him down. He gathered this information through a continuous process of self-analysis. Today, he doesn't reference it much anymore—it is simply a statement of who he is. Now he knows.

A personal vision of prosperity compelling enough to spark the passion to make it happen has to come from within. You can't define that vision until you "know thyself." Why? Let me repeat my definition of the *state* of prosperity: an existence that enables you to apply your passions, personal strengths, and values to work that is personally satisfying and fun while providing the financial resources to experience your envisioned life. If you don't know what your values and strengths are, how can you spot or create opportunities to apply them?

The Power of Being Self-Aware

What are your values? What are your strengths? What are you good at? What do you most enjoy when it comes to people you spend time with, the work you do, the organizations you work with or for? If you can align your world with these realities—as much as possible—you'll find yourself speeding through iterations of the Prosperity Cycle.

Don't be afraid to look in the mirror! The problem most of us face is that we're so afraid of admitting our faults we avoid self-analysis and so never have the opportunity to really understand our strengths. And that is a prosperity killer. We are many times more productive—which breeds success—when we are operating within our strengths and passions—which breeds fulfillment. In fact, renowned psychologist and expert in talent development Travis Bradberry wrote in his book *Emotional Intelligence 2.0*, "As self-awareness increases, people's satisfaction with life—defined as their ability to reach their goals at work and at home—skyrockets. Self-awareness is so important for job performance that 83 percent of people high in self-awareness are top performers . . . Why is this so? When you are self-aware, you are far more likely to pursue the right opportunities, put your strengths to work and—perhaps more importantly—keep your emotions from holding you back."[3] Bradberry interviewed approximately 500,000 people in his research on emotional

3. Travis Bradberry and Jean Greaves, *Emotional Intelligence 2.0* (TalentSmart, 2009), 26.

intelligence, so I tend to trust his statistic. In a similar study of 1,000 entrepreneurs, Bill Wagner, author of *The Entrepreneur Next Door* (Entrepreneur Press, 2006), identified self-awareness as a critical characteristic of successful entrepreneurship.

In practical terms, increased leverage of your strengths and values results in a level of performance that is sure to get you noticed in almost any environment. Understanding who you are and applying yourself accordingly is a great way to differentiate. Top performers make more money and get more promotions or are more successful as entrepreneurs. More important, they are happier and more fulfilled by their work. The ability to leverage every talent, every strength, every value, every passion small or large will make you prosperous every day because your work and life will be satisfying and fun.

Becoming cognizant of what you excel at can also be your ticket to engage the Prosperity Cycle—the catalyst that forces you to make a decision to finally do something. Internalizing your unique competence makes you painfully aware of situations in which you aren't able to engage your talents. It helps you understand why you are dissatisfied. Recognizing this can provide the impetus to "decide" to make a change, to kick off the Prosperity Cycle. Making changes to what you do and where you do it in order to better align your work (or studies) with your strengths is a primary shortcut to prosperity. When you do this, you are striving for a compelling personal vision, one in which you are wholly satisfied.

But how do you develop the necessary self-awareness?

Values

Why do you like something or not like it? Why do you feel comfortable in some situations and not in others? Often, answers to questions like these come down to the set of values you've developed over time that make you the unique individual that you are.

Often times we aren't even aware that we have developed these values and would be hard-pressed to list them. Instead we feel the presence of them by how a situation makes us feel. Let's say that you and a colleague are in sales and are pitching a product to a potential buyer. Your colleague promotes the product in a way that is factually accurate but purposefully misleading. If that gives you the heebie-jeebies, then you can be sure that you have a well-developed sense of honesty and integrity, even if you've never thought about them as core values.

Where do our values come from? We tend to absorb the value systems that are most dominant in our current environment. The younger you are, the more likely that they come primarily from your home environment and your parents in particular. And those values may stay with you for the rest of your life. But as you get older you may also be influenced by your teachers, bosses, and peer group. That is why it's important to choose your friends, mentors, and advisers wisely, and the environments you learn, work, and live in carefully.

You aren't going to feel prosperous if you have to spend time every day with people who aren't aligned with your values or in an environment that isn't aligned with your values. Traci Fenton, founder of WorldBlu, an organization dedicated to promoting democracy within organizations, tells a great story about her first realization that her value system wasn't aligned with that of many companies, particularly the first one she worked for out of school. Her strong belief in the value of helping people live to their full potential clashed with their command-and-control culture.

"To support myself after graduating from college and to gain some practical experience while starting WorldBlu, I took a job with a small division of a Fortune 500 company in the Midwest. I quickly met with the harsh reality of the slow dehumanization of people in the workplace each day, the limiting of their potential. Four months later, I resigned. *Jerry Maguire*–style, I presented my boss with a manifesto of freedom. I told him in no uncertain terms that this wasn't how anyone should be treated in the workplace. What did he say? 'I knew you were too smart to let yourself be treated the way we treat people here.' Unbelievable. But over the next few days, two managers resigned too. It seems I wasn't the only one who saw the flaws in their system."

That experience pushed Traci to focus even harder on building WorldBlu, which she had started in her college dorm room. Organizational democracy, she believes, is a system that helps people live their full potential. Over the last fifteen years, she has created the WorldBlu List of Most Democratic Workplaces™, building best practices with companies like Zappos, DaVita, Great Harvest Bread Co., New Belgium Brewing Company, Orpheus Chamber Orchestra, Podio, WD-40 company, and many others—companies with cultures that honor the same values WorldBlu holds. She has become a renowned speaker on the subject and is writing a book entitled *Freedom at Work* on the benefits of organizational democracy to both organizations and individuals. I'm not sure I could have contrived a story better than this one to explain how important our values can be in determining the right path. If you wonder if Traci feels prosperous, watch her TEDx talk.[4] You can't fake that kind of passion if you are unhappy in what you do.

---

4. "TEDxMadtown - Traci Fenton - WorldBlu, Democratic Workplaces," TED—Ideas Worth Spreading, last updated April 28, 2011, tedxtalks.ted.com/video/TEDxMadtown-Traci-Fenton-WorldB.

Traci isn't the only person on the planet who has let her values drive her career choices. Look at founders of organic food companies or Peter Thum, a McKinsey consultant who, once exposed to the dire lack of clean water in South African communities, founded Ethos water. Five cents of each bottle sold is used to support clean water initiatives in underdeveloped communities.

So what are your values? And how do they impact your daily fulfillment and your long-term plans? To help you identify the values that need to be a part of your work or life experience in order for you to be fully engaged, committed, and happy, try the exercise shown on page 61. You can also fill it out online at www.shortcutto prosperity.com.

If you completed the exercise, you now have a short list of values that are important to you. That's invaluable, but you're only partway there in terms of really getting to know yourself. Remember, over time, your values can change. This is an assessment you need to perform more than once, and particularly when you're considering a major life change.

Strengths

The second step in knowing yourself better is to determine what you are good at. I'll use the term strengths, for simplicity's sake, but you might use talents, aptitudes, or something else. It doesn't matter what you call them. What does matter is whether or not you are using your strengths every day. If not, I doubt you feel very prosperous.

Tom Rath, author of *StrengthsFinder 2.0*, has shown (through Gallup Organization research) that people who focus on their strengths every day are six times more likely to be engaged in their

Identifying Your Personal Values

Following is a fairly comprehensive list of personal values for you to consider.* Start with the first one and imagine spending time every day (at work or home) in an environment that doesn't include it. How would it make you feel? If it seems impossible to you, put a checkmark next to it and move on to the next. Then reread the list of those you checked and eliminate those you feel less passionate about than some of the others. Keep doing this until you get to a list of about six. If you are struggling to narrow the list, try thinking about a time in your life when that value was very important to a decision you made or in how you acted or reacted. If you can't think of one, it might be one to eliminate. If this list is missing a value that has meaning for you, add it to one of the blank lines.

__ Accountability	__ Forgiveness	__ Leadership	__ Self-discipline
__ Beauty	__ Freedom	__ Learning	__ Self-expression
__ Choice	__ Generosity	__ Love	__ Self-reliance
__ Collaboration	__ Gratitude	__ Loyalty	__ Self-respect
__ Commitment	__ Happiness	__ Merit	__ Serenity
__ Community	__ Harmony	__ Modesty	__ Service
__ Compassion	__ Health	__ Nature	__ Simplicity
__ Competition	__ Honesty	__ Optimism	__ Spirituality
__ Courage	__ Hope	__ Order	__ Sportsmanship
__ Creativity	__ Humility	__ Patience	__ Stewardship
__ Dignity	__ Humor	__ Patriotism	__ Thrift
__ Diversity	__ Idealism	__ Perseverance	__ Tolerance
__ Empathy	__ Independence	__ Pride	__ Tradition
__ Enthusiasm	__ Individuality	__ Privacy	__ Truth
__ Equality	__ Innovation	__ Prudence	__ Wisdom
__ Excellence	__ Integrity	__ Resourcefulness	_____
__ Fairness	__ Interdependence	__ Respect	_____
__ Faith	__ Justice	__ Responsibility	_____
__ Family	__ Kindness	__ Security	_____

* "List of Personal Values," Personal Legacy Advisors, accessed July 15, 2012, www.personallegacyadvisors.com/knowledge-base/downloadable-values-list.

jobs (or studies) and three times more likely to report having an excellent quality of life in general. It makes sense, right? We all like to do what we are good at, and the ability to do so on a daily basis should lead to a higher level of personal satisfaction—and a greater sense of prosperity.

Consider the Prosperity Cycle graphic on page 19. If you are applying your strengths in a focused effort to achieve a goal, you will absolutely see a return on your investment of energy. You are far more likely to be successful, even in small ways, which helps you build confidence and persevere. Even if you fail, if you are leveraging your strengths, you are more likely to walk away from the experience having learned something valuable. If you are expending a lot of energy and applying focused effort in a way that isn't aligned with your strengths, the cycle is going to be slow. It will take you a long time to see results, you'll get frustrated, and you may give up altogether. Understanding and leveraging your strengths are critical steps to getting the most out of your efforts, to keeping the Prosperity Cycle running smoothly. And more often than not, your strengths are tied to your personal vision of prosperity in some way.

If you are over age twenty-one and are still doing work that you don't much like, it's high time you did something about it. Developing a better understanding of your strengths is an important step in the right direction. And if you're in any kind of leadership position, you aren't responsible for understanding only your own strengths. The most successful leaders build their teams based on a finely tuned understanding of what strengths are most crucial to getting the job done. Leveraging the strengths of the people on their teams to their highest use, these leaders are able to achieve incredible goals.

When I use the word strengths, I'm not talking about skills ("I'm good at using this software program"); I'm referring to personality or behavioral-based aptitudes ("I'm good at learning new skills under pressure, like new software or new systems"). It's nice to understand the minutiae, too, but when you're trying to make a decision to go down one path or another, you often don't know what the minutiae will look like. What you probably do know is whether you'll do better in a certain career or situation because you're flexible and are good at adapting to quick changes or whether it requires somebody who is more analytical and able to develop multiple plans and strategies based on possible future events.

I mentioned *StrengthsFinder 2.0* above, and it's a fascinating tool for better understanding your personal aptitudes. The book summarizes the work of a forty-year Gallup research effort to identify the thirty-four most common human talents. For the price of the book, you get free access to the online assessment tool that will give you a twenty-page report that identifies the strengths most dominant within you, describes the general characteristics of each strength, and offers personalized insights based on how you answered the questions.

When I took the assessment, I found that the themes for my strengths were Futuristic (inspired by the future and inspire others with my vision), Strategic (create alternative plans to proceed in any given scenario by spotting patterns), Maximizer (stimulate personal and group excellence by transforming something strong into something superb), Individualization (intrigued with the unique qualities of each person and how people who are different can work together productively), Achiever (a lot of stamina and take great satisfaction from being productive).

Understanding what's not on your strengths list is almost as important as recognizing what is. A talent in discipline, for example, means that you enjoy routine and structure. Me? Not so much. I made a major breakthrough in my organization's productivity and in my personal happiness when I quit trying to make myself provide routine and structure—something that our organization desperately needed but that I found exhausting. Realizing that there were people who enjoyed structure as much as I enjoyed developing strategy was huge. Eventually our organization adopted a hiring process called Behavioral Interviewing: You figure out what strengths are required by a position and then look for past behaviors in candidates that show they enjoy doing what the job requires. Learn to do this for yourself in order to ensure that you apply only for positions that require strengths that you have.

Even though you probably won't be entirely surprised by the strengths identified for you, the tool gives you a structure for thinking about your strengths and specific recommendations for how to capitalize on them.

While I think this is a great tool, a host of other ways can help you to think about your strengths. Other assessments, like the Myers-Briggs Type Indicator or the DiSC Profile, focus on personality inventories that can help you understand basic traits. The book I mentioned above, *Emotional Intelligence 2.0*, also offers a free assessment of your emotional intelligence. These types of assessments also help you understand your strengths, in a way, although how you interpret these tests and what you do with the information is just as important.

What's most important with any of these tools is that you don't let any one of them, or comments from any one person, define your view of who you are or what you're capable of. You might learn that you are more likely to do well with a regular and predictable routine, while somebody else might yearn for frequent change and variety. It's just one dimension of who you are, though.

And ten years from now, it might be a bit different. As Steve Jobs once said, "Don't let the noise of others' opinions drown out your own inner voice. And most important, have the courage to follow your heart and intuition. They somehow already know what you truly want to become." You can change certain things about your life and even about yourself, and others you shouldn't try to change. All of these tools simply help you develop a better understanding of where you are right now. If I had taken the Strengths-Finder assessment thirty years ago, would I have gotten the same results? Probably not. Our experience shapes us and forces us to grow in ways we may not have thought possible.

You might be thinking, what about weaknesses? Are we going to talk about those as well? Nope. A growing body of research supports the wisdom of working to develop the strengths you already have a natural affinity for rather than striving to eliminate your weaknesses. While you can work to minimize your weaknesses, it will be slow going and not a lot of fun. The same level of effort targeted at building on your strengths will not only be a lot more fun (and so sustainable) but will also yield a much higher return in terms of growth. And building on your strengths will help you naturally overcome some weaknesses that are fundamental enough to hold you back.

Many of the shortcuts in this book could be considered strengths, but I believe they are actually learnable behaviors that exist in some as strengths. They are foundational enough that everybody should be able to master them at some level. You'll be stronger in some than in others, and that's fine. It just takes a bit of effort in each area to build the habits and skills that will keep you on your personal road to prosperity.

Write It, Record It, Ponder It

The recommendation to keep a journal (or a personal blog) is one of the most heartfelt that you will find in this book. And it's easy—because, if you are like most people, you are your own favorite subject. It is simply a matter of making the time to do it. And I'm not alone. Sir Richard Branson, Chairman of the Virgin Group, uses his journal to keep a record of projects and ideas he has while he is on the move and recently posted an urgent blog request asking for help in finding his misplaced journal.

I started keeping one when I was in college, thanks to a recommendation from a friend. In retrospect, I can say I learned more from my journals than I did from any other source. Because, for me, the most valuable knowledge was the self-discovery of what I liked, what I was good at, what was important to me, and ideas on how I might go about pursuing what I wanted. I was learning enough about how the world worked from my studies and the people around me. What I really needed to know, and couldn't learn any other way, was how *I* worked. And my journal helped me rediscover that well into my professional life. Eventually I used the journal to determine that I got bored in every job I ever had. And that helped me realize that the rigorous pace and constant new challenges faced by an entrepreneur could be a good fit for a guy like me. And then in 1995, the year before I started Peak Industries, I wrote the following:

Things I like:
- *Building, expanding*
- *Investing in an asset, paying it off, and reinvesting*
- *Improving, as in redesigning, something for improved cost or performance*

- *Providing great service*
- *Directing people*
- *Ownership and true responsibility*

Things I'm good at:
- *Speaking, effective communication, persuading*
- *Analysis and choosing the right course of action*
- *Identifying excellent performance when I see it*
- *Comprehending technology*

Start a journal. Find some dead time in your schedule and start using it to document what you are thinking about—what you are learning about yourself. Airplane time, commute time, contemplative Sunday afternoons are all great times to make a few notes. Keep your journal handy to use to capture insights and ideas as they happen. I put this toward the end of the shortcut because your journal is a great place to capture self-learning, whether you are thinking about your values and strengths or are even contemplating your own "I Am" document. Because if you can become more self-aware and reconnect with your internal compass, you'll be able to tap all of the energy you need to create a prosperous life.

Entrepreneurs chase dreams—their own dreams. They are unwilling to settle. They understand what prosperity means to them and are unable to imagine living any other way.

That is why knowing thyself became such an important shortcut as I developed the ideas behind this book. At first, I thought it seemed a little soft. But if you can't define your personal vision of prosperity or it's not true to who you are, there is no point in pushing forward.

The goal of this shortcut is to consider how you work, how you interact with others, how you communicate, what type of work environment invigorates you, and how you manage stressful situations. You can then take these insights into account as you tackle major challenges or make important decisions. You want to reacquaint yourself with your internal compass, your gut, that helps you make smart judgments.

Take what you've learned about yourself and use it as a jumping-off point to develop a clear, practical vision for where you want to be, something I'll help you do in the next shortcut.

Finding the Shortcut

- Review the times in your life when you felt incredible—like anything was possible. What had you just done? How did you do it? What personal strengths helped make it possible?

- It can be just as valuable to be honest with yourself about the things that you are capable of being good at and perhaps are required to do by your current job but that you really don't enjoy doing. School and early career experience teaches us to excel at whatever we are told to do. The rest of your life is too short to fill with things that you can do well but don't enjoy doing. What are you good at that you don't enjoy?

Do Something

- Start a journal this week. It could be a document, e-mail you send to yourself, a blog, or a notebook. I know one person who even tackled it by writing e-mail to his newborn son.

Those e-mail messages helped him explore his values and what he believed about the world. However you do it, I guarantee that it will be incredibly helpful in bringing your shortcut to prosperity into focus. Find the time, and start capturing your thoughts on who you are and what you want. Add an appointment to your calendar right now!

- Take the StrengthsFinder 2.0 assessment this week. A validation code for the test comes with the purchase of the book, or you can just pay for the assessment online at strengthstest. com. It will use the results of years of research to identify your top five talent themes along with ideas for how to leverage your particular strengths.

SHORTCUT 4: Build Creative Tension

We all know the speech.

> I believe that this nation should commit itself to achieving the goal, before this decade is out, of landing a man on the moon and returning him safely to the Earth. No single space project in this period will be more impressive to mankind or more important for the long-range exploration of space . . . If we are to go only halfway, or reduce our sights in the face of difficulty, in my judgment it would be better not to go at all.

With these rousing statements, President John F. Kennedy set the country on a path to do something that, at the time he gave the speech, was impossible. The technology to make it happen did not exist.

Now, Kennedy didn't simply throw the idea out to the country without a clear sense of what he was asking. "[No project] will be so difficult or expensive to accomplish," he said. "Let it be clear that I am asking the Congress and the country to accept a firm commitment to a new course of action, a course which will last for many years and carry very heavy costs." In fact, the first American had been sent into space just three weeks prior to the speech. But Kennedy was so clear-eyed about what it would take that he carefully mapped the investments and innovations required to bridge the gap between where the space program was and where it needed to be. Funds to accelerate the development of spacecraft, funds for engine development, funds for unmanned missions to make the eventual manned mission as safe and successful as possible, $23 million for the development of a nuclear rocket, $50 million for satellites to support worldwide communications, $75 million for a satellite system for worldwide weather observation, an additional $7 to $9 billion invested over the next five years—these were just the biggest hurdles the program faced.

Despite the massive distance and numerous hurdles between the space program's current reality and future vision, they achieved exactly what Kennedy set them on a path to achieve. On July 20, 1969, eight years after the speech, the first manned spacecraft landed on the moon.

Of course, that is not the end of the story. The focused drive for a goal resulted in a period of technological innovation that shaped the next forty years and continues to influence our lives every day. We have cell phones because of NASA-inspired communications satellites. We have early warning weather detection systems. We use a mouse to interface with computers. We have patient health monitoring systems in hospitals. The list is vast. So vast, in fact, that NASA launched *Spinoff*, a journal focused on highlighting the transfer of NASA technology to the private sector—and our daily lives.

On the way to a clearly defined goal, our country has benefited in innumerable ways, but that goal would not have been attainable without the analysis of exactly what it would take to get there. Kennedy and his team built *creative tension*—tension created by clear understanding of current reality and a specific vision for the future.

And if they could use creative tension to pull the country toward such an immense goal, you can certainly use it to achieve your vision.

The Power of Creative Tension

Hewlett-Packard and Emerson Electric both leveraged tools developed by MIT professor and author Peter Senge in their leadership training programs. Senge built on the work of his friend and colleague Robert Fritz to show that people who take the time to develop a compelling personal vision, and who see clearly the changes necessary to achieve the vision, are highly motivated to make those changes.

Let's make this real. Imagine stretching a rubber band between your left and right hand—or pick up a rubber band and do it. Let your left hand represent your current reality and your right hand represent your personal vision. Fix the position of your left hand by internalizing every aspect of where your life is *right at this moment*. Fix the position of your right hand by imagining your life as you would like it to be *ideally*. Now think about what it will take to get from your current reality to your vision and move your right hand away from your left to reflect that effort. Feel the tension in the rubber band—the tension between your vision and your current reality—trying to pull your hands together. You have only two choices to relieve the tension. You can do what it takes to move your current reality toward your personal vision or give up on your vision and convince yourself to be more satisfied with your current reality and the status quo. While nothing is wrong with either approach, most readers of this book are attracted to a force that drives change for the better.

That is what creative tension offers. When you are clear-eyed about where you are right now and have a specific personal vision that you hold in your mind, you'll feel the tug every day, pulling you closer to it, helping you make smart choices, helping you accept the changes that may be necessary. A deeply meaningful personal vision finds its way into your daily thoughts and actions, modifying your behavior and bringing energy and enthusiasm to every attempt you make to change.

Music educators Rosamund Stone Zander and Benjamin Zander, authors of *The Art of Possibility* (Penguin, 2002), understood this concept well when they developed the idea of "giving an A." Benjamin Zander teaches at a conservatory, and with every new class, he watched students limit their development as musical performers because they were so worried about competing with their classmates for top grades. Rather than focusing on taking risks and growing in their abilities, they played it safe—and limited their potential in the process.

His solution? On the first day of class, he announced that at the end of the year, he would give each of them an A. He had one requirement. Each student had to write him a letter, postdated for the end of the year, explaining in detail what he or she had done over the past ten months to earn the A. He told them specifically, "I am especially interested in the person you will have become by next May. I am interested in the attitude, feelings, and worldview of that person who will have done all she wished to do or become everything he wanted to be" (27). He described the A as "not an expectation to live up to, but a possibility to live into."

The result was astonishing. The students' letters presented moving, powerful personal visions for the accolades they would earn and the competitions they would win, the moments of insight and mastery they would achieve, and the musicians, performers, and people they would become. And the students then used those personal visions to transform themselves.

In 1995, I was thirty-six years old. I had married the love of my life, and we had two daughters, ages three and five, who I thought were just about the coolest kids ever. Our two-engineer income enabled us to live in a house of our own design overlooking the lights of Fort Collins from the foothills that rose along the west side of town. And while I knew that I had a great life, I had also achieved a lot of the goals I had set for myself, and it was time to stretch, to paint a picture of what I wanted my life to be like. My value and knowledge had a shelf life, and what I wanted from life would never be more achievable than it was right then.

So, in my journal, I described the kind of world I wanted to live in and the kind of life I wanted to lead for the rest of my time on earth. It was pretty aspirational stuff. I wrote about a happy, productive world "free of avoidable pain and suffering." I wanted to have an identifiable role in helping build such a world. I wanted a loving and easy relationship with my close family. I wanted a successful business in a community where we would want to live as a family. Toward the end of my list, I started getting more practical and specific. I wrote that by the time I was fifty-one, when I hoped both kids would be in college, I wanted to be financially independent, and I wanted to be the owner/operator of a company with $40–$80 million in revenue.

That plan is almost exactly what ended up happening. (The world isn't free of pain and suffering, of course, but I am involved in activities and organizations that could help create a better world.) I don't think it was a coincidence that I achieved much of my vision. It happened because I was able to assess my current reality and develop a compelling personal vision, which built the creative tension necessary to make it happen.

Now, if you did the rubber band exercise, you might not have found much tension in your rubber band. In other words, your vision isn't far from your current reality. It's an expression of how satisfied you are with your current life. Being satisfied is important. You want to enjoy what you've accomplished. But a fun, exciting, prosperous life is also full of potential and growth. Don't let satisfaction in the moment or with the minutiae limit your vision for the future. Give yourself an A, and then develop a plan for how to get there.

Developing Your Personal Vision

When it comes to developing a vision, Steve Jobs didn't always get it right. In the 1980s, he thought he wanted a "professional" CEO to guide Apple while he focused on the creative process of product development. He didn't know what a pain in the rear a CEO could be, especially one who didn't necessarily share his vision. John Sculley ended up firing Jobs from his own company. Jobs may not have *wanted* to be CEO, but a more careful investigation of his personal vision, in terms of what he really wanted to achieve, might have told him he *needed* to be CEO. It would be ten years before Jobs had a chance to correct this mistake.

For most of our lives, unless we're playing it very safe, we are navigating the unknown. We never know what might happen next. A personal vision is the most basic of compasses. It can keep you headed inexorably toward your ideal, prosperous life instead of wandering aimlessly or getting stuck on an unsatisfying path. Without a personal vision, the amazing life you vaguely dream about is unlikely at best. With a personal vision, it's a specific, achievable goal.

You might believe, like many people, that the world dictates the situation you now find yourself in and that you can either accept it or be bitter about it. Frankly, that's a load of bull. In fact, you can shape your life into almost anything you want it to be. Can you start a new career track? Absolutely. Can you go after that promotion? Yep. Can you go back to school? Why not? Can you do something more meaningful with your time? Please do!

Your vision is the prize. It's what you think about when you're hauling your butt out of bed in the morning, when you're pushing through a long day, when you're tackling one more challenge, and when you're having fun doing it. You just need to take the time to think about what you want, what you really want, and then write it down and internalize it. The result will be a creative tension that starts working for you, pulling you toward the vision you created.

Your personal vision is a series of statements that define what you want your life to look like, feel like, and be at some future point. It will cover everything from identifying your ideal line of work, to how you will integrate your values and strengths into your everyday life, to the material things that you want, and everything in between. Your dreams of achieving an economic or leadership pinnacle, of being a better servant to others, of fostering stronger connections with the people in your life are all components of prosperity.

Your vision is influenced by the person you are—your values, strengths, and passions—so the work you did in shortcuts 2 and 3 creates a great launch pad. Consider what you've learned about yourself so far as you work to develop a clear vision. And let me offer some advice for the rest of the process. Find a quiet place where you can think without being interrupted. If you are more relaxed and open minded while listening to music, fire up a favorite playlist. I'm old school and still think better with pen and paper, but it will be easier to refer to your notes later if you do it on your laptop or tablet. You can go to www.shortcuttoprosperity.com and download a template. Now follow the instructions in the exercise, which is based on Peter Senge's book *The Fifth Discipline*.

Personal Vision Exercise

Imagine yourself at some point in the future, perhaps five years from now. You've worked hard to engineer a life that is incredibly rewarding. You are doing work that is satisfying and fulfilling, and you look forward to each new day. You've earned a sense of well-being—you are content with your home life, professional life, your relationships, and your self-image. You earn an income that suits your lifestyle. Using the following prompts, describe how your life looks and feels. Use the present tense to describe it. If these categories don't work for you, invent your own. And spend more time on the elements that are most important to you.

Work
Describe what you do for a living. What kind of a company do you work for? Do you work alone or with a team? What are your responsibilities? Describe anything you can about the type of work you do, why it is valued and by whom, and how it allows you to leverage your values and strengths.

Home
Where do you live? What does your home look like and how is it a good fit for you? The more details the better.

Relationships

Describe the important people in your envisioned life. Spouse? Family? Friends? Business associates? Pets? How will they help your life be more fulfilling? How do your values play out in your relationships with them?

Health

Are you healthy, fit, and full of energy? What do you do to achieve that? How do you manage stress? How do you maintain a positive outlook?

Self-Image

How do the important people in your life describe you? Why do they treasure the opportunity to work with you, hang out with you, or love you?

Fun

What are the activities that recharge your batteries or give you satisfaction outside the work environment?

Tangibles

It's OK to put voice to the things you want in your life, even the material things. They help make your vision real. How much money do you make? How much money do you have saved? What things do you have that are important to your lifestyle and your enjoyment of life?

Community

What do you do to give back? The successful people I know gain as much (or more!) satisfaction from helping others.

Faith

This may or may not be part of your personal vision. If faith is an important part of your life, then you should include it in your personal vision. How do you plan to observe your faith in your envisioned life?

Life Purpose

For most people, this is the toughest question. Write down some thoughts about the essence of what you are here to do and what you would like your legacy to be. Elements of this are woven through your answers to the previous questions, so don't worry if you don't have a distilled purpose statement.

Suspend judgment about what you "should be" including in your vision and write down whatever is personally motivating. If the idea of having a house on the water or a Porsche in the driveway is motivating, then by all means include it. If it will fuel your internal fire, it belongs in your vision. But be prepared for the fact that this process will require some trial-and-error iteration, because sometimes what we first imagine doesn't actually reflect what we really want. It's just a reflection of the path that we're on right now.

I will also tell you with conviction that some of the most satisfying human experiences are those that are selfless. Your personal vision is a living document, and over time I think you will find that it includes more ideas for helping others at work, in your community, and in your family.

A good way to sort out some of the chaff is to ask yourself, "If I could have this right now, would I take it?" When you consider it from that perspective, some things won't make the cut. Say, for example, you took my advice to dream big and imagined that you would be driving a Ferrari. If you actually thought about the stress of driving that car, the agony of parking lot dings, the outrageous insurance, and what else you could have purchased instead, you might take it off the list. But if you're a car buff, you might decide that it would all be worth it. Or say that you imagine working for your competitor in a better position, but when you think about it, you realize it isn't a great idea because you actually hate the industry you're in. You may imagine having six kids. When you stop to consider what it would be like to live in a house with six kids right now, you may change your mind. Having lived with two, I can imagine how tough it would be.

Another good filter is to dig deeper on the elements of your personal vision to find out if they are just proxies for what you *really* want, another great idea from Peter Senge. Assume that you have achieved a certain element of your vision and ask yourself, "What does that bring me?" For instance, I had a lake house in the life plan that I wrote when I was thirty-five. When I asked myself this question, I realized that my vision wasn't so much about the house but about what happened in the house. What I really wanted was a place where my family and friends could gather, a place that would help us stay close as my girls grew up—one that would provide a host of shared and precious memories. I ended up with a townhome near a ski area. Sometimes you have to ask yourself this question a few times to get to the real heart of what it is you want.

A final method for testing your vision is to say it out loud, maybe even to another person. If you can't own it, you won't achieve it. It's weird—saying something out loud shouldn't change it that much, but it does. Imagine if the leaders of a company developed a vision for amazing growth and progress but never told the rest of the employees. What's the chance that vision would come to pass? The first time I went through this exercise, I was dating Jenny, who would become my wife. I used her as a sounding board for my personal vision. It helped me figure out what I believed and what I didn't, what was real, and what was overly idealistic. She was also honest with me about what elements of the vision sounded like the Mark Hopkins she knew. She helped me believe I could achieve the vision simply because *she* believed that I could.

If you already have a vision but it isn't compelling to you, you haven't stretched your imagination enough. Your vision should be so big that a part of your brain is saying, "No way. I could never do that," while another part of your brain is already starting to plan the steps on that path. Your internal voice should say, "How cool would that be?" and "Why not me?" A powerful personal vision should be both exciting and terrifying at the same time. Work on it until it is, and don't worry about its being too big. We'll talk about how to tackle it step-by-step in shortcuts 5, 6, and 7. Even if it doesn't come to pass or you decide to change it, you've put yourself on a path that is true to who you are and that will bring you closer to prosperity than you are now.

If you haven't done the personal vision exercise in earnest yet, please, please put it on a "to-do list" and do it! I can't stress enough the need to develop creative tension in your life, and you can't have creative tension without a compelling vision and an honest assessment of current reality. The sooner you get started, the better.

Assessing Your Current Reality

The power of creative tension comes from the honest assessment of the distance between where you are now and where you want to be. It's not nearly as exciting to acknowledge your current reality as it is to develop your vision, especially if you aren't satisfied with where you are. But it is a necessary part of the process. In order for the personal vision to have meaning, you have to view it in relation to your current life. If you don't know where you are, how can you chart a course to where you want to be?

In general, I am a huge proponent of maintaining a positive, glass-half-full worldview. If someone asks me how I am, I always answer with "Super!" or "Terrific!" It helps my energy level and also pumps up the people around me. But get ready to lose the rose-colored glasses and be brutally honest. An unrealistic assessment of your current reality will only serve to undermine the creative tension that you are trying to discover.

Most of us struggle to be honest with ourselves about our current reality. It's not our fault, really. It's a survival or coping mechanism. If things in our lives are bad, our minds can work very hard to avoid reality and develop an outlook that we are in a different situation than we actually are, even that we are different people than we are. It's like the alcoholic who can't acknowledge that he has a problem. The reality is obvious to everybody else but not to him.

Anything that you deem important enough to be a part of your personal vision needs to be honestly assessed as part of your current reality. To bring this down to earth, if it is important to you to teach in some capacity, it becomes relevant if you realize that you are in a job that offers no opportunity to do so and no chance to get on that path—your reality and vision are pretty far apart. If you want to feel strong and energized, it becomes relevant that you exercise every day—your reality and vision aren't far apart at all. Part of your current reality is simply who you are, which you explored in the previous shortcuts.

To help you through the process, I've developed the exercise shown next, which mirrors the personal vision exercise. It is important to be as specific as possible. As you complete this exercise, do your best to be honest about where you are right now in life. After you've become clear about the reality, consider what changes you will have to make to get from where you are to the ideal you described in the personal vision exercise.

Creative Tension Exercise

Using the following prompts, describe how your life currently looks and feels. Be brutally honest. If necessary, involve other people and ask them to help you answer some of these questions. If these categories don't work for you, invent your own. And spend more time on the elements that are most important to you. Then, in each category, describe the changes that you would have to make happen to transform your current reality into your envisioned life.

Work

Describe: What do you do for a living? What kind of a company do you work for? Do you work alone or with a team? What are your responsibilities? What values and strengths do you apply in your work? Do you give it your all every day? Do you like your job? Is it fulfilling? Why or why not? Describe anything you can about the type of work you do, how you feel about it, and how it is valued.

Transform: Based on this reality, what changes would be necessary to get you to your personal vision?

Home

Describe: Where do you live? What is your home like? Is it a good fit for you? How do you feel when you walk in the door?

Transform: Based on this reality, what changes would be necessary to get you to your personal vision?

Relationships

Describe: Who are the important people in your life. Spouse? Family? Friends? Business associates? Pets? Do your relationships make your life more fulfilling?

Transform: Based on this reality, what changes would be necessary to get you to your personal vision?

Health

Describe: Are you healthy, fit, and full of energy? What do you do to achieve that? Do you manage your stress? Do you maintain a positive outlook? How?

Transform: Based on this reality, what changes would be necessary to get you to your personal vision?

Self-Image

Describe: How do the important people in your life describe you? Why do they treasure the opportunity to work with you, hang out with you, or love you?

Transform: Based on this reality, what changes would be necessary to get you to your personal vision?

Fun

Describe: What are the activities that recharge your batteries or give you satisfaction outside the work environment? How often do you do them? Why do you enjoy them?

Transform: Based on this reality, what changes would be necessary to get you to your personal vision?

Tangibles

Describe: How much money do you make? How much discretionary income do you have after all of your bills are paid? What is your net worth? Are you saving money for the things you want in the future? What things do you have that are important to your lifestyle?

Transform: Based on this reality, what changes would be necessary to get you to your personal vision?

Community

Describe: What do you do to give back? Does it bring you a sense of fulfillment and purpose?

Transform: Based on this reality, what changes would be necessary to get you to your personal vision?

Faith

Describe: If faith is important to you, how do you observe it? What role does it play in your life?

Transform: Based on this reality, what changes would be necessary to get you to your personal vision?

Life Purpose

Describe: Do you feel that you are fulfilling your life purpose? Not to be overly morbid, but if you died tomorrow, what would your legacy be?

Transform: Based on this reality, what changes would be necessary to get you to your personal vision?

This exercise may have been particularly hard for you. Sometimes, being honest about your reality really sucks. Who wants to admit that they've got too much debt, that they're in a job they don't really like, that they need to lose twenty pounds, that their relationship with their family isn't great? These are hard facts to swallow. But once you face it and own it, you can move beyond it. What keeps most of us comfortable with the status quo is our fear of facing the realities. It may seem daunting, but it is the most valuable first step you can take toward any kind of change in your life.

If you are like most people, you are not satisfied with your current reality and have a lot of ideas for what you want your future life to be. We all get to define *prosperity* as we see fit. Some of our definitions will mean that there is quite a distance from our current reality to our personal vision. Before now, you may not have been very specific about either. The exercises in this chapter can help you generate massive transformational energy by building creative tension.

This exercise, like the process of understanding your talents, is often the impetus behind making a decision to do something. The compelling personal vision is crucial, but it's the understanding of how far you are from it and what will be required to get you there that actually gets you off your butt. And don't fear if the distance between your vision and reality seems vast. The rest of this book is designed to help you develop the skills and behaviors that will reduce that distance, step by running step.

Tough Trade-offs

You may have found that one change necessary to achieve different aspects of your vision is a change in your financial situation. If you want to travel extensively *and* save money for your kid's college education *and* go back to school to change your career path, you'll need the financial resources to make those things happen. And reaching a certain financial goal in order to lead a certain lifestyle may be an important part of your vision. Your vision is your vision; there are no judgments here.

But I offer some hard-earned words of advice. I know a lot of people who have been incredibly successful financially. Every single one of them has learned this lesson: The pursuit of more and more money doesn't equate to happiness. Happiness is a function of being actively engaged in work that you perceive to be of value, having a loving relationship with friends and family, and living a life that is in concert with your values. You just have to balance the need for certain resources with a vision that is deeper and broader than simply acquiring those resources.

You may need to also consider a host of trade-offs as you develop your vision and the plan to get you there. Take the example, "I would really like to double my salary." In your career, doubling your salary may mean traveling half the month and catching up on paperwork on the weekends. If your personal vision also includes spending more time with family or pursuing an athletic challenge to see how far you can push yourself, the new job may make your other goals impossible. Of course, you may find ways to negotiate these trade-offs, opportunities in the world that will let you have it all. Maybe it's time to take the plunge and leave the safety of your current job for one that offers more money without additional sacrifices. Test the components of your plan by making sure you will be getting what you actually want—not just five years from now, but all along the way toward your goal. The journey has to be exciting and enjoyable.

If you have done the work to develop a meaningful personal vision and have been honest about your current reality, you deserve both congratulations and condolences. Congratulations because, probably for the first time, you know what prosperity means for you. Condolences because you now know how much work it is going to be to get from here to there. But fear not, the next two parts of the book provide guidance on how to shorten your path to prosperity and how to enlist the help you will need to get there.

Finding the Shortcut

- Creating a personal vision is an ongoing process. When you have clear, long-term vision elements in place, you may only need to review them periodically. But if either you or your environment is changing rapidly, your vision can get out of alignment quickly. Inevitably when I'm feeling a little off and don't know why, I discover that my personal vision is out-of-date. Keep this in mind when you decide how often to update it. Start with quarterly and go from there.

- Pursuit of an effective personal vision will keep you looking for the life experience that allows you to move toward it. Your path will be a lot shorter if you can get this at work. Finding a boss that gets it and is supportive of helping you to get the experience your vision requires is priceless. Find one that does and stick with her for as long as you can.

Do Something

- Complete the personal vision, current reality, and transformational statements that are contained in this shortcut. Don't turn the page until you have set a day and time to take a first pass! Here's a hint. Avoid being overwhelmed by keeping your transformational statements short and measurable. Don't worry that some can be achieved in a few weeks while others may take years.

- Write down the most outrageous personal vision element that you can imagine—the one that you would never tell anyone else. If you think you can do it, you're not thinking big enough. Take that piece of paper and put it someplace safe. Just writing it down and keeping it will change your perspective of what's possible.

- Once you've developed your personal vision, post it on this book's website, www.shortcuttoprosperity.com. You can choose to keep it anonymous, but putting it up for the world to see will still inspire you to make it happen.

Develop *an* Unfair Advantage

SHORTCUT 5: Learn from the Best People and Organizations

Craig Wickersham was a young man walking alone on a beach in Carmel, California, the day he saw the house that set him on a path to becoming the most joyful person I interviewed for this book. Craig saw a house emerging from the seaside cliffs. "It grew from the site in a way that left me feeling as though it was meant to be there—that it had always been there." Later he discovered that this was exactly what Frank Lloyd Wright, the home's architect, had intended. Wright once said, "Nature is my manifestation of God. I go to nature every day for inspiration in the day's work. I follow in building the principles which nature has used in its domain."

Craig was blown away by the communication of natural harmony and intention through architecture. In the design of that house, he found his passion.

Craig discovered his passion early. He was thirteen when he saw the house in Carmel. Shortly after, he designed his first house, and by fourteen, his first home design was under construction. Throughout high school he apprenticed with architecture firms in Scottsdale, Arizona, but he understood that to even hope to achieve the inspired architectural design that Wright mastered, he had to do only one thing—learn what that master had to teach. At the very young age of seventeen, he arrived at Taliesin West, the Frank Lloyd Wright School of Architecture facility that began as Wright's home in Scottsdale. He was accepted on the spot. Craig studied under Ling Po, one of Frank Lloyd Wright's most gifted apprentices, digesting architectural concepts and insights in a matter of years that Wright spent a lifetime exploring and perfecting. Don't get me wrong; Craig has committed thousands of hours to learning his trade, but the architectural wisdom that he had amassed at the age of twenty-five allowed him to produce designs that many architects would not be able to duplicate at any age. Craig leveraged his passion for and exposure to the teachings of one of the masters in the field to become an outlier in terms of his age and skill level.

Malcolm Gladwell describes the process that transformed Craig in his book, *Outliers*. Gladwell estimates that it takes 10,000 hours of focused effort or practice to become world class at something, from computer programming (Bill Gates) to hockey (Wayne Gretsky). At the heart of the 10,000-hour requirement is a concept called learning-curve theory that industrial engineers have used for over a hundred years to predict how much faster a person will get as they repeat the same task over and over. My analytical, engineering brain loves this kind of thinking. For example, a learning curve for a particular task might predict that it can be completed with 10 percent less labor each time the cumulative number of task completions doubles. In other words, as you complete a task for the second time, fourth time, eighth time, and so on, you can expect it to take you 10 percent less time. A task that takes you an hour the first time you do it will take you thirty-nine minutes the sixteenth time you do it. The exhibit shows a graph of this learning curve, called the 90 percent learning curve.

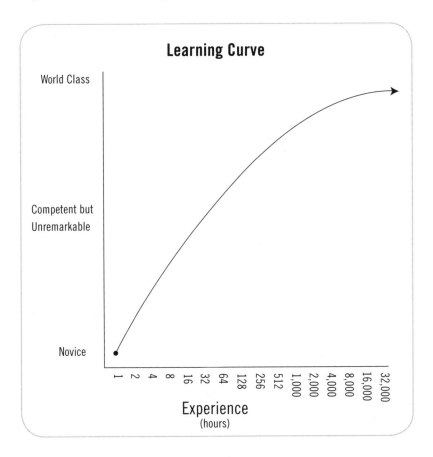

You can see that after 10,000 repetitions (hours) the curve gets flat and the potential for further improvement is limited. According to Gladwell's research, this is the point on the curve where individuals of incredible talent operate. They aren't quite as good as they could ever be, but compared to people operating early in the curve, they appear to be gifted geniuses. This is why finding your passion by indulging your curiosity is an absolute necessity. Without the passion, it's hard to make the commitment necessary to get to that point, or very far up the learning curve at all.

Experience (and a lot of it) is how you gain the knowledge you need to set you apart from the crowd. It's essential to working your way up or leading your own company or achieving your personal vision. But . . . *but* there are shortcuts to earning this level of experience. Daniel Coyle calls them *hotbeds*, places of training and coaching and learning where knowledge and talent are grown at a surprising rate. Taliesin provided just such a hotbed for Craig, demonstrating why learning from the best can be a shortcut to prosperity.

What the Best Have to Offer

Innovation: Whether you're entrepreneurial or not, you need to understand it. In most situations and for most people, prosperity springs from ideas that are new, different, and better, from people thinking creatively about a problem and solving it. That's what innovators do. They *add value*. While creative thinking is necessary to innovation, so is learning. To be an innovator, you have to be exposed and open to new ideas, new ways of doing things, and particularly best practices. The better the sources of information available to you, the faster you'll learn and the more experience you'll gather in shorter periods of time. Sometimes trial-and-error learning is your only option, but when it isn't, when somebody else has already gone through that process and knows what you need to know, why struggle along, learning the long and hard way?

This is the key distinction between effort and focused effort. The former might not push you toward your vision or keep your Prosperity Cycle going; the latter most definitely will. Focused effort is required to win or to ensure that, if you fail, you learn powerful lessons along the way.

You will move much faster along the learning curve and give your Prosperity Cycle more fuel if you align yourself with great organizations and people who are pursuing passions similar to yours and who can teach you what you need to know as quickly as possible. You will learn from every person and every organization that you spend time with. What you learn may be positive or negative. You may develop a resilient mindset, a sense of integrity, and knowledge of the best ways to get things done. Or you might learn to do things half-assed, to do only what's asked of you, and to take the easy way out. If you are working on the wrong stuff or learning bad habits, it's going to take a lot more than 10,000 hours to achieve the expertise you want. When you're working in a hotbed of success—surrounded by world-class practices, people, and organizations—you work on the right stuff at all times, dramatically shortening the time to personal excellence. That is why this shortcut is titled "Learn from the Best," not "Learn from Just Anyone."

What you see done becomes possible. Once you're convinced something is possible, you're just a few steps from making it reality. History is full of examples of unimaginable milestones—like the four-minute mile—that, once achieved, are quickly achieved again and again. Position yourself in a hotbed where impossible things are being done, and you'll find yourself doing impossible things, too. Most successful entrepreneurs surround themselves with people they can learn from, not only before they launch a company but also as they strive to grow it. Education and idea exchange are the founding principles of organizations like Entrepreneurs' Organization and Young Presidents' Organization that exist to share proven best practices with its membership.

Learning from the best is also a great way to test the strength of your passion. Some people go to law school only to find out that they don't like being lawyers. Some people get onto a career path that they realize isn't a good fit, sometimes not until it's difficult to make a change. But if you can gain exposure to a field, particularly through some of the best in the field, in some capacity, before investing 10,000 hours in it, you may save yourself time, money, and effort.

And the most wonderful thing about this shortcut is that you actually have access to the best, sometimes the best in the world. Warren Buffett once said, "I won the lottery the day I emerged from the womb by being born in the United States instead of in some other country where my chances would have been way different" (Alice Schroeder, *The Snowball*, Bantam, 2009). I couldn't agree with him more. The United States offers a combination of basic rights, learning institutions, innovative corporations, and inspirational icons that, when combined with our egalitarian nature, creates a platform for prosperity that is unequaled anywhere else in the world. The UK-based *Times Higher Education* ratings of universities shows that the United States has seven of the top ten institutions and seventy-two of the top two hundred worldwide. Many of the world's leading companies are based in the United States—from technology innovators to restaurant chains. The sheer size of our GDP alone means that you've got a better shot at learning from within a strong, growing company and developing a profitable career here than in any other country in the world. And did you know that it takes 120 days to get through Brazil's bureaucracy to start a company? And in Suriname, 694 days? At best this is due to a poorly designed legal system and is more likely indicative of a corrupt system that favors insiders and the established. In the United States, the process takes only six days.

Everything you need to learn and to achieve your vision of prosperity is at your fingertips. You just need a plan to leverage it.

Choosing the Right Place at the Right Time

So often, we look at people who are successful and lead prosperous lives and think, "Well, he was in the right place at the right time, wasn't he." This may be true, but it wasn't luck that put him there. We all make choices every day that put us in the path of opportunity. Two of the biggest choices we make in terms of advancing our learning curves are where to go to school and where to work.

Learning 101

Your career is like a two-stage rocket. Your formal education represents the first stage. It doesn't last very long or move a rocket very far, but it gets the craft moving and helps it break away from gravitational forces. And at any point in time, you may need to use thrusters, relying on education again to shift your direction or propel you forward.

Is college really necessary? Not if you're like Steve Jobs—fortunate enough to have found your true passion by age eighteen and have already developed or found a path to the expertise you need to begin your career without college. For the other 99.9 percent of you, keep reading!

College, graduate school, and other forms of continuing education can help you escape the gravitational force that is the status quo. We are all pulled toward a life and career that is familiar. The best college experience is one that exposes you to as many new ideas, new experiences, and new perspectives as possible. These will help you break the status quo in your mindset and then escape the status quo in your life.

You can apply the whole learning curve concept only when you know what you are interested in, and a formal but flexible learning environment is a great place to pursue a lot of ideas, to indulge your curiosity. Don't be in a hurry to define a path if you aren't sure. Use educational opportunities to safely explore your options before deciding what's best for you.

That said, a bad college experience is one that leads you through or into a subject that you are not passionate about or one that requires you to take on a debt level that is inconsistent with the level of income that graduates of that program can typically expect to generate. Instead, look for the educational path that gives you the best value (a good ratio of marketable skills and connections to the cost of the program).

A good college experience should teach you how to think critically, how to communicate effectively, and how to solve problems efficiently. These are essential skills for being both a lifelong learner and an innovator—and they're in high demand at the best companies.

The Right Job for Maximum Learning

The right job can be a huge shortcut to prosperity. A successful, established company has not spent 10,000 hours figuring out the best way to accomplish the tasks that are central to its business model—it has invested *hundreds of thousands of hours* figuring it out. And to stay viable, it will keep investing time and money to find ways to do what it does better. The leaders' job one upon hiring you is to teach you those hard-earned lessons. If you love what you do and love the company you work for, it can seem almost criminal to be paid a salary to learn the secrets of its success.

Of course, you have to also face the reality that not every job, particularly the first job you take that puts you on a certain path, will be glamorous, high-paying, and constantly fulfilling. Sometimes, to get into the best learning environment, you have to make sacrifices—grunt work, a pay cut, a job that is tangential to what you think you really want to do. In the end, though, if the learning opportunities are there, it will be worth it. Read on to understand what to look for.

An ideal job at the right organization will give you an opportunity to refine your ideas and your passion. You may feel passionate about a general industry or type of work or area of study, but career paths become more specific than that. And going to work for a successful company that will invest in your development is an amazing way to find the niche within an industry that is most appealing to and the best fit for you. If you don't like it there or you're bored right away, you probably won't like it anywhere. Better to get off that path quickly and onto the next. Learning from the best allows you to confirm your passion and explore its depth and breadth in a world-class environment—an environment that is aligned with where you want to go and can help you get there faster.

I was a kick-ass student as an engineer at Cornell University because I worked hard. What I got in return was the right to go to work for Hewlett-Packard, one of the most respected innovators in the world at that time. It also earned me the right to request a job in Colorado rather than Vancouver, Washington, where they wanted to send me. It had been my dream to work and play in the champagne powder of the Rockies. I spent the next three years working hard and playing harder. Mechanical engineering tools used during the week were traded for skis, dirt bikes, and boats on the weekends.

During this time, I learned something important. I didn't like mechanical design. Being chained to a CAD system and rarely talking to anyone else wasn't for me. I gradually shifted my emphasis to technical challenges that involved coordinating people, projects, and other facilities. Every activity was based on a work process and system that was the result of tens of thousands of hours of effort by HP to figure out the best ways to do things. Without even knowing it, I was leveraging HP's learning curve, absorbing efficient approaches to everything from project management to organizational structure. They even had a name for it: The HP Way.

After a few years I was promoted to a leadership position and started in on a whole new learning curve. I attended a series of training classes to help me maximize others' productivity and encourage them to do their best work. And when my responsibilities and the growing computer business required me to develop processes and systems that didn't exist at HP, I attended a new program at Stanford University that would help HP lead the way in global computer manufacturing. I spent the next year, at HP expense, earning a master's degree and learning the skills that would be the basis for the company I would found later. Of course, this was also a win–win for HP. I used what I learned there to lead the implemention of a state-of-the-art global computer manufacturing control system that gave HP a competitive advantage in the industry.

Is the (only slightly more) modern workplace different from

my experience? Not much. Exchange Google or Apple for HP and you still have a leading company looking for hardworking and educated young people to help move their organizations forward.

In short, they are looking for the people who embody the skills promoted in this book. Anyone exhibiting these skills is in the driver's seat in the job market and can afford to be selective in terms of the organization he or she chooses to join.

The list shown here will help identify companies that will offer the best learning opportunities for you.

Of course, it would be ideal to find a company and a job that offered every one of the attributes noted here. But those jobs are few and far between and the competition for them is fierce. Instead, you may have to focus on those attributes that are most crucial to you based on your personal vision. If you are focused on becoming an exceptional leader, you should be sure to identify companies that are known for developing exceptional leaders and have exceptional leaders who mentor others. If you are just starting out on a new path, identifying opportunities that are well aligned with your vision at companies that are high growth (opportunities for faster promotion) may be quintessential. If you need to gain industry knowledge rapidly, look for market leaders. You may need different opportunities at different points in your career, and so you should prioritize these attributes of great companies accordingly.

If you have recently redefined your personal vision, ask yourself what the first job is that you need to get to put yourself on the path to that vision. It may be your current job or a job at your current company, and it may not be. If you have a day job that you're relying on to earn a living and are exploring your passions at night and on weekends, it could take a long time to learn what

Characteristics of a Company You Want to Work For

Alignment

The company's core business should be in the area that you have the most interest in (refer to shortcut 2), and the position should be one that works to your strengths (see shortcut 3) and provides opportunities to move you closer to your personal vision.

Market Leader

The company should be a leader in its primary market, in terms of market share, innovation, or some other key measure. Market share leaders work long and hard to create a business model, hire great team members, and develop products and systems that will earn them a spot at the top. Market innovators leverage knowledge to make big advances. These are the types of companies you want to learn from.

High Growth

High-growth companies create more opportunities for their employees, and often develop new and interesting positions that allow you to explore different aspects of how the company and the industry work. You'll usually be ready for your next challenge before your employer is ready to promote you into it. But at a high-growth company, you often won't have to wait long. Plus, a high-growth environment is just more exciting.

A Reputation for Developing People

Great companies don't just put you in a job and forget about you. They understand that they are building relationships with their employees, and those relationships should be growth oriented and win–win. They make it okay to be up front about where you want to go (personal vision) and help you identify opportunities where their business needs align with your developmental needs. The best of the best will wish you luck when your continued development means that you have to move on.

A Great Boss

The right boss is like a great teacher, helping you to see the forest for the trees and making the process of learning fun and interesting. The right boss alone can cut your learning time in half by ensuring that you are practicing the right skills and executing the skills right. The best way to identify a great boss is by talking to her subordinates. They'll show gratitude and fanatic loyalty if their boss is doing right by them.

you need to learn. It's better to find a way to get inside the leader's organization, even if it means making some sacrifices.

Remember that the learning process is dynamic. At some point, personal growth can stall out anywhere you are. Be prepared to move when your learning slows down or the organization you work for moves in a direction that doesn't work for you. Even a great company can be a lousy place to work if you aren't able to make progress toward your vision. When what you need and what they need is aligned, stay; when it isn't, it's time to move.

While I was still at HP, I started to dream about the company I would eventually start. I had known for some time that becoming an entrepreneur was a primary goal. Unfortunately, I had no idea how to do it. I recognized how ill prepared I was for what I envisioned. While I had a good engineering and production background, I had never had financial management responsibility or experience in critical areas like sales and marketing or strategic planning. It would take years to gain the experience I needed at HP, if I ever got it at all. I was learning from the best, but only in a narrowly focused engineering management role.

If I was going to pursue my vision, I needed a new job that would offer opportunities to learn different skills. A recruiter in Chicago put me in touch with Emerson Electric, and I was offered a job as the vice president of manufacturing for a division in Boulder. I would get the experience I was looking for. My move paid off. In 1996, after six years with Emerson, I developed a plan to leave and start Peak Industries, a medical device manufacturing company that leveraged my deep knowledge in manufacturing technology within a niche that I saw as underserved by the competition. I would get the chance to live my dream of becoming an entrepreneur and creating the work environment that I yearned for and hoped that it would attract other talented people.

Each learning experience with a company or job will push you forward. Shannon Deegan, the hockey player I told you about in chapter 1, is a great example. He spent two years as a special assistant for trade and foreign policy to the future prime minister of Canada, where he learned that the work ethic he learned in hockey translates to any endeavor. That led him to spend three years as chief of staff and senior policy advisor on Asia for the secretary of state of Canada, learning how to communicate and sell ideas by making them personal and creating win–win opportunities. That led him to become assistant vice president of business development in Asia for London Life International and then director of business development for Manulife Financial, where he learned that you can repurpose the platform of knowledge you've built and that you should say yes to opportunities whether you think you're entirely ready for them or not. That led him back to school to earn his MBA at Yale University, where he learned foundational concepts of business analysis and strategic thinking. That led him to a position with McKinsey & Company, the world's most respected management consulting firm, where he identified his interest in media and technology and learned how to provide his skills to clients. That led him to launch his own consulting company, where he learned to be entrepreneurial and developed the confidence to leap into the void. That led him to become director of sales operations and business planning for Yellow Media, where he gained more depth in media and technology. That led him to Google, where today he is the director of people operations and has learned to maximize his personal success by surrounding himself with talented people and offering them the growth opportunities they covet.

Get a job with a market leader (or as close as you can come to it) operating in the space that you are interested in and ride up their learning curve. You will come out of that experience years ahead of your peers and ready to take a shot with a smaller company, where you might be able to rise even faster. It might even be your own.

Pursue the Passionate, Avoid the Zombies

Whether we like it or not, we become more like the people we spend the most time with. It's our human nature, helping us adapt to fit in with the social environment. That powerful instinct can be used for good—or evil. Well, not necessarily evil, but who you choose to spend time with can affect your learning curve and, consequently, how prosperous you become.

Now, I'm not trying to sound elitist. I'm not saying, "Only hang out with rich people and you'll get rich too." And I'm not encouraging social climbing for the sake of social climbing. What I am saying is that you should admire the people in your life for their determination, for the knowledge they've acquired, for the values they live by, and for their efforts to achieve their own personal vision of prosperity. To be prosperous, you need authentic, meaningful relationships that help you learn about yourself, your world, and how to win. Achieving prosperity can be tough, and it happens a lot faster if you are inspired and are learning the right habits. If you look around at the people in your life and you see a lot of complaining and not a lot of well-planned decisions or focused effort to create a meaningful life, you may need to think about spending time with some different people.

As the song goes, we've all got "friends in low places," and we shouldn't abandon those friendships. They can be incredibly meaningful to us and keep us connected to who we are. But if you *only* have friends in low places, it means you're spending most of your time in low places too, that you are likely developing a "low places" attitude and mindset. That's not going to help you achieve what you most desire.

In order to learn everything you can to achieve your vision, you need to surround yourself with people who are on fire, people who are well into the Prosperity Cycle. This is true of friends and even romantic relationships, but it's especially true of colleagues or partners in any of your goals (like an exercise or study partner). The goal is to accelerate learning while making it fun. Being with people you like who are also skilled and prosperous allows you to almost effortlessly develop the same skills that make them successful. The transformation happens through osmosis.

Actually, according to Joseph Grenny, Kerry Patterson, and the rest of the authors who contributed to the book *Influencer*, a key step in changing our behaviors is changing our minds about those behaviors: whether they are desirable or not, what kinds of outcomes they deliver, how risky they are, and so on. Through extensive research, what the authors found is that the primary way to change minds is through personal experience. If you believe something that isn't accurate, and then through personal experience discover that your thoughts were wrong, your mind will be changed. The next best thing to personal experience, though, is what the authors call *vicarious experience*. Watching others experience success through certain behaviors or hearing stories of how they succeeded by leveraging certain behaviors will help ensure that your mind is open to adopting those behaviors.

If you want a shortcut to prosperity, look for people with a sparkle in their eye and a spring in their step. They are constantly exploring, wondering, and have already done things that you haven't even thought of. They are innovators, and they have a healthy disregard for rules or push the limits just to see what happens. They are doing interesting things in interesting ways. Some of them will be bosses or teachers, but more of them will be your peers. Glenn, Charlie, Alex, and a host of others have served this role for me. We worked together, did really stupid things together, and over time expanded our view of what was possible. They became lifelong friends. They became my informal board of directors in the business of life. I wouldn't be who I am or have achieved what I have without them. Make sure you find yours.

These are the people from whom you will learn the most and who have the potential to offer you great opportunities. You probably already know who some of these people are in your life, but here is a list of attributes to help you spot those already on their own paths to prosperity.

People You Should Learn From

The proactive
Those who are designing their life with a plan in mind

The goal-oriented
People who constantly give themselves something to work toward and a way to build a sense of accomplishment

The passionate
People who exude energy and ideas, and follow them through to achieve great things

The curious
Those who are constantly exploring and learning, who are multifaceted in their interests, and who enjoy sharing what they've learned with others

The unconventional
Those who are innovators, who ignore the naysayers, who make their own paths

The connected
People who may know other people whom you could turn to for career advice or help

Steve Goldman, whom you will hear more about in shortcut 9, found an amazing group of people to learn from in college—a relationship that has continued for more than twenty years. After joining a fraternity his freshman year at the University of Michigan, he lived off campus with twelve fraternity members who shared his penchant for thinking outside the box. In between their studies and parties, they did plenty of creative thinking about topics of interest to college students, the most common of which was how to earn spending money. (One of the most enterprising of his roommates identified a campus demand for sporting wagers and set up shop briefly as a bookie.) "Have you thought of this?" or "Can you top that?" were questions often overheard in the house. They slowly changed the way they thought about what was possible and left school with open minds and a can-do attitude. Over the course of fifteen years, they left a high-water mark in business success that would be tough for any other group of twelve to equal. Among other things, they:

- Founded Moosejaw Mountaineering, a chain of stores with tens of millions in sales dollars and an award-winning Internet outlet that combines serious mountaineering equipment with a zany attitude.
- Founded Crowdrise, a website that uses crowdsourcing to assist in charitable fundraising.
- Founded Workforce Insight, a $20 million service company that helps large organizations like Walmart maximize their investment in workforce management technologies.
- Founded Kurtzman Carson Consultants, a company that

developed software to automate the bankruptcy process, which was sold to an industry leader in a nine-figure deal.

- Founded PaySimple, an accounts receivable software service developed to simplify the process of collecting receivables for small business owners.
- Became principals at leading private equity and financial service firms.

These guys still keep in touch, providing advice and encouragement to their friends' enterprises, each a little in awe of what the other is doing.

I can't overestimate the power of the peer group. When you can, avoid the naysayers, the reactors, the uninspired, the at-all-costs rule followers, the brain-dead. And don't become one of these people. Be upbeat, engaging, and open. Invite interaction with your attitude. The more you can wear a smile, the better. Replace cynical comments with a good-natured sense of humor. Be the person that everyone is happy to see.

We all lead incredibly busy lives, and if you want to be proactive and shift how you are investing your time, pursuing relationships so that you can learn from the best is one of the easiest, most enjoyable, and leveraged opportunities for creating a shortcut to prosperity.

Earn the Opportunity to Learn

Going to college, getting a job with a great company, and spending time with amazing people are all great starts for developing learning opportunities. But once you're in these environments, you have to prove to the people around you that you are ready and eager to learn. Here are some ideas for putting yourself in the path of learning opportunities.

Say Yes!

People (managers, professors, entrepreneurs, coworkers, teammates) are always looking for help. You can either be the person who looks at the ground when somebody is looking for help with a new project or you can be the one who says, "I'll do it!" Volunteering builds your reputation as someone who is always up for a new challenge and buys you more one-on-one time with the people you can learn the most from. And when you do this with your boss, you also become a good candidate for the next promotional opportunity. If you find that the last thing that you want is more time with your boss or you aren't learning much from people you work with or other teammates, then you should think carefully about your situation and changes you might want to make.

If you see an opportunity, don't wait for somebody to ask for help. Volunteer, especially for teams or assignments that may be above your pay grade or slightly above your skill level. Seek out the best teams and do what you can to work with them. The best learning environment is one in which we are forced to stretch ourselves.

Why should you take on new work? Mostly to keep from getting stuck in a rut. We are creatures of habit, and it is easy to find yourself completing the same tasks day after day, improving your skills but possibly not learning new ones or developing new insights. Adding something new increases learning and introduces the chance for an integrative experience (cross-fertilization) where the new activity allows you to think differently about things you already know. You also might find something you love doing more than your current assignment. Better yet, new experiences put you in touch with new people, expanding your personal network and potentially leading to a great opportunity.

The only caveat with this approach is to make sure that you don't overcommit. You can still volunteer if your plate overfloweth, but make sure to ask your boss to help you prioritize your workload. Having said that, this recommendation works best for those who are okay doing a little extra work. The Shortcut to Prosperity is only a shortcut if you are willing to do the work that most aren't.

Don't Be Afraid to Ask

The type of people you have the most to learn from are likely to get great satisfaction from helping others and sharing what they've learned. Don't be afraid to ask for help or to ask questions. It's not nice to pester people, but respectfully asking for advice or some wise education on how to tackle a problem will show people that you are open to ideas and feedback. Be prepared to give something back, however. You can turn a one-off interaction into an ongoing relationship by offering to do background work (perhaps market research) or by tackling other tasks in your strike zone. You may even have a background that allows you to offer something of unique value to somebody whom you admire. In the best case, you could find yourself pursuing an opportunity that you couldn't have previously imagined.

Take It on the Chin

In order to learn from the best, the best have to be willing to teach you. Much of the "teaching" is going to come in the form of constructive feedback—personal feedback on things that you do well and probably even more on things you don't do well or knowledge that you don't have. The right mindset (open and accepting) makes it easy for your more experienced colleague to give it to you straight. And this is exactly the way you want it if you want to get down the learning curve as quickly as possible. If you have a tendency to avoid criticism or to shrink from feedback, you might want to revisit the growth mindset (versus fixed) that I described in shortcut 2. Learn to embrace criticism and the more experienced person providing it in order to shorten your path to the level of knowledge that leads to prosperity.

And remember, no one likes the cocky kid. It's much more enjoyable to be around the confident but modest professional whose performance and winning attitude make it clear that she is the real deal.

The essence of this shortcut is the understanding that prosperity requires deep knowledge in the area of your passion, and that the most potent form of learning comes from people and organizations that have more knowledge than you do. The best part about it is that learning is really pretty easy. I have no doubt that ample opportunities are in front of you every day to grow and learn and find new shortcuts to achieving your vision. It's just a question of whether you are seeking them out and taking advantage of them.

If you find yourself being cautious, holding back from taking on new challenges because you're worried and think that you might not succeed, the next shortcut is for you.

Finding the Shortcut

- Ask yourself if you are passionate about the work you are

currently doing. If not, is your lack of passion indicative of a misfit with the market space or just because you've stopped learning?

- Start thinking of every interaction as an opportunity to learn. Managers, colleagues, friends, suppliers, and customers all have knowledge that you need. Even random interactions can be mined for knowledge that is on your path to prosperity. Instead of making small talk, make it a game to figure out someone's expertise and learn something from every interaction!

Do Something

- Based on your thoughts on the first question above, take action today. If you aren't interested in the market space, congratulate yourself for figuring this out and find a new employer in a different market. If you aren't learning, you aren't getting closer to your personal vision. Find out if your current employer faces a challenge that offers an opportunity for you to advance your personal growth. Draft your next Prosperity Cycle and find work that enables you to complete it.

- Identify someone you know who is incredibly talented at something and ask how he or she got so good at it. Ask a few people. You will find that their paths included thousands of hours of hard work fueled by a passion for what they became good at and guidance from a more experienced practitioner (coach). Take any specific tactics that you heard from them and apply it to something you want to learn.

- Make a list of people you know whom you would like to learn from and think of ways to spend time with them. It might be through a formal mentoring relationship or more likely through a more informal process such as grabbing lunch or a beer after work. Make a conscious choice to spend time with people who are inspirational and who enjoy idea exchange.

SHORTCUT 6: Earn an "I Can Do Anything" Attitude

I grew up in a small town of about seventeen thousand people—Anywhere, USA. Everybody knew everybody, of course. But in our middle school, one boy was particularly well known for a unique talent. His name was Mike Cooney, and I was lucky enough to be his friend.

Like most middle schoolers, Mike was driven by a social motivator: He wanted to be admired by his peers. And what draws the attention of twelve-year-old boys, other than girls and video games? Bodily functions. Crude, but true.

So Mike became a master belcher.

Mike would swallow mouthful after mouthful of air until you could actually see his stomach distend. When he could swallow no more, he would let go, producing the loudest, longest, most revolting sound imaginable. He turned heads and rattled windows. His abilities were legendary. I looked at Mike then as I look at Warren Buffet today—in a class by himself.

Unfortunately, the admiration Mike received came only from other boys. Girls and teachers? Not so much. And even among us boys, Mike's skill became less admired as we got older. So Mike moved on to develop other talents.

You are probably wondering what belching has to do with success and prosperity. Prosperity, no matter how you define it, isn't an instantaneous leap forward. It starts early and it starts small. With each success we achieve, our confidence grows. We leverage that confidence to help us achieve our next, greater success.

That is the definition of an "I can do anything" attitude—confidence in your ability to tackle the next challenge and turn it into a spectacular opportunity. Confidence that has to be earned and built over time. And that is why I thought of Mike.

Mike is extraordinarily successful today, enjoying a prosperity that he built over the years, one success at a time. In high school, he did well academically and on the lacrosse field, earning a spot on the roster at Cornell University, where he played on two Ivy League championship teams. After he graduated with a finance degree, he developed his career at Merrill Lynch, Bear Stearns, and Deutsche Bank. Eventually, he was asked to open a new Boston office for UBS Securities and then to do the same as managing director for Merriman Curhan Ford & Co., a securities broker and investment bank.

Did being a great belcher really put Mike on the road to success? It's hard to say (but I wouldn't recommend adding "belching" to your résumé). What I do know is that it gave him an opportunity to excel at something, and sometimes that's all we need to get started. Mike's odd ability helped build his confidence, a confidence he relied on as he developed other skills and talents. From there, every additional win in the classroom or on the field gave him the leverage to aim higher and higher, setting bigger and bigger goals. And they helped him weather the tough times and pitfalls that occur in life as we grow and stretch our abilities.

Earning an "I can do anything" attitude is the result of successive achievements of increasing magnitude, or in other words, iterations of the Prosperity Cycle. It's that simple. This might seem like a chicken-and-egg conundrum, but it isn't really. Competence breeds confidence, bit by bit, in different aspects of your life at different points in time. Win or lose, each lap around the Prosperity Cycle builds confidence, preferably through the euphoria of having worked hard at something and experiencing the payoff, but confidence is also built when someone with a growth mindset appreciates the learning that occurs when results don't meet expectations. Some cycles are bigger than others, but they all help you map your world and make you more confident that you know how it works.

Earning confidence early and often is a shortcut to prosperity because we have to be able to step off the beaten path and blaze new trails to be truly prosperous.

Confidence in Your Vision

Go big or go home!

Man, I love that phrase. It's a perfect reflection of the nature of prosperity. More important than accumulating money or "things," prosperity is the act of living our dreams, achieving big goals, earning a sense of accomplishment, contributing to the world around us. Yes, financial rewards often go hand in hand with meaningful accomplishment, but they may not. Consider teachers in inner-city schools, people who start up new nonprofits to better the lives of others. Are they in it for the big bucks? Not likely. They are following their passions, fueling their internal fires. That said, many people who develop the skills to achieve at the highest levels often end up making a pile of money *and* helping make the world a better place. It isn't an either/or and you shouldn't feel guilty about wanting to do both.

Confidence, that "I can do anything" attitude, is essential for going big, regardless of the nature of your personal vision. Living a prosperous life means creating a vision that has meaning to you and reorganizing the world to make it a reality. That "reorganizing" often means taking a risk, going out on a limb, and especially breaking away from the herd. A herd mentality is unlikely to help you achieve your goals.

Think about it as an economic equation. More often than not, the return on investment for an action taken as part of a group is diluted in proportion to the number of people making it happen. Group actions and goals are based on what is best for the entire group. They are arrived at through consensus and compromise. Occasionally, you'll get lucky and your goals will align perfectly with those of a particular group, or the group will want to head in the direction that your personal plan requires. When that happens, take advantage of it. But it is rare.

What is more common is to find yourself generally moving closer to your goals, but on a less than direct path. Or in worst-case scenarios, being pulled by the herd away from your goals. The only way to recognize when this is happening is to have a clear picture of your personal vision. And the best way to remedy it—the shortcut—is to break off on your own when the opportunity presents itself, to make an entrepreneurial move, to imagine, create, and pursue your own path. And that takes confidence.

Being a pioneer is scary. Leaving the safety of a group is scary. Doing something that may or may not be successful is scary. To make matters worse, we humans are naturally inclined to point out people who are different, who are doing something "crazy," and disparage them. And deep down we all know it. We feel it. With this knowledge, how are you supposed to summon the courage to strike out on your own?

Before you can *do* anything, you need to *believe* that you can do it. Courage has to be learned. A growth mindset has to be learned. You have to learn to take risks. And you have to learn to accept failure and move on. In my life, I've learned to look at everything that doesn't go as I had planned as an opportunity— to experience something new, to find an even better solution, to discover a better path. Life presents us with so many hurdles, so many moments that could be seen as small failures, and that's why it's essential to develop this attitude.

Of course, life also offers many moments of success. Recognizing and leveraging your past successes makes you less reliant on the security of a group, particularly when you have had to overcome steep challenges to accomplish them. You can feel confident in your ability to handle the unforeseen circumstances that will arise. You are more willing to take an unknown path if you have done it before and succeeded.

Of course, it helps if you've had successes to build on. So let's start there.

Earning It

Your personal interests, life experiences, and motivation combine to determine what you get better at and where you find success. Of course, some of our early demonstrations of competence aren't very marketable. But remember, it starts early and it starts small.

Each time you put yourself out there, striving for a goal, four important things happen:

1. You learn something valuable and advance your quest; you complete another lap around the Prosperity Cycle.
2. You discover the exponential power of hard work. As you work harder and harder, your results grow exponentially. Other people might call you lucky or clever, but you know the truth.
3. You fail in small ways and big. And learn that that's okay.
4. You realize that it feels great to succeed! Moments of independent success, even small ones, are like an addictive drug—a positive addiction to the actions that drive your life toward prosperity.

Most of us read of others' accomplishments in the news and think that there is absolutely no way that we could ever achieve what the all-stars do. That is partially because what we mostly hear about are the outcomes, not the step-by-step growth that went into achieving the outcomes. If you're thinking about a major success as one giant step, you're right, it's never going to happen. Great accomplishments are the result of a long series of less-than-great accomplishments, and failures. But with a few exceptions, almost anything you want to do, you can. You have to really want it, you have to be willing to work hard for it, and you need the patience and perseverance to take it step-by-step. With each step, your competence and confidence will grow, making the next step easier and more exciting.

But how do you get started? The highest level of confidence often begins very humbly, maybe by being good at something that only a niche group values (twelve-year-old boys, for instance) or even that only you and your family value.

Take It Step by Increasing Step

Consider a goal in your personal vision. Now, identify a very achievable milestone on the way to that goal, something you can tackle soon and simply. It might be something as basic as making an appointment, blocking time on your calendar, or contacting somebody who could help. It's important to jump in but also to be realistic. Focus on that first milestone. When you get there, set the next one in your mind, but make it a bit more challenging. And so on.

This obviously isn't rocket science. It's Training 101. But it is science, the science of psychology. Renowned psychologist Mihaly Csikszentmihalyi developed a concept for the optimal experience of finding true happiness in the challenge of progressive improvement. Think of those moments when you are using your skills to their fullest and then pushing yourself just a bit harder to reach a goal. Those are the moments in life that bring us the greatest happiness and fulfillment, because we become wholly engaged in the activity. In fact, his research, described in his book *Flow*, showed that it does not matter how grueling, repetitive, or mundane the task. If you can focus on leveraging your skills or talents to improve your performance, you can enter a state of flow. Tackling a challenge that requires skills that we have, but at a slightly higher level, helps us focus our mental energy, our attention, which results in being completely absorbed by the activity. When clear goals are established (like beating a certain time or doing a job just a bit better) and you get immediate feedback, it encourages you to renew your focus, to become even more absorbed. To get technical, our consciousness, which is limited by the central nervous system's ability to process only so much information at one time, becomes more orderly, and the information that is being processed is more aligned with our goals in the moment. Everything we are doing and most of what we are thinking is focused on reaching the goal. And that orderly connection of consciousness to action to goals breeds enjoyment and happiness. To understand the idea better, you might read Professor Csikszentmihalyi's book.

The idea I'm trying to sell here is that achievement is a lot of work but ultimately doable, and the sooner you teach yourself to do it and enjoy it, the sooner you will achieve your next big goal. For instance, any able-bodied person can run a marathon. Period. Hundreds of websites offer gradual training schedules that, if followed, will allow you or anyone else to run a marathon. If you aren't currently a runner, the first milestone might be walking three miles four times in the next week. The following week, the milestone might be to jog for at least a quarter mile of your three-mile route. The next week, make it a half mile. Before you know it, you'll be jogging three miles. Now add a mile. And another. And another. Before you know it, you'll be jogging five miles, and then eight, and then ten. It's simply a matter of putting in the time. But each new mile will give you a sense of accomplishment that will spur you on to the next mile. And when you complete a marathon you will have done something that 99 percent of Americans have never done. Why? Because it is a lot more work than 99 percent of the population wants to undertake.

There was a time, before we had kids, when my wife, Jenny, and I were really into seeing what we could accomplish athletically. We started small with a 5K turkey trot at Thanksgiving, worked up to 10K runs, and eventually completed a half marathon. But those early successes served only to whet our appetite. So we trained for and completed a marathon and then began reading about triathlons. One brisk morning, we were enjoying a ride in the foothills west of Boulder and had just stopped in a clearing to feel the sun on our faces. Clearly under the influence of an endorphin-induced high, Jenny wondered aloud what it would feel like to complete an Ironman. I think I said, "Are you crazy?" I know I thought that anyone who would swim 2.4 miles in open water, bike 112 miles through the mountains, and then run a marathon was out of his mind. But you can probably guess where this story is headed. The beginning of a new Prosperity Cycle had been initiated, almost as if I had no choice in the matter. Two summers and a thousand or so training hours later, Jenny and I completed the Canadian Ironman and discovered just exactly how cool it felt.

I took away so many important lessons from this experience. The first was that, even though completing the Ironman was almost unimaginable when Jenny and I first started running 5Ks, we were both perfectly capable of doing it. We just had to take it step-by-step. The second was that continuous improvement is an incredible motivator. We were training with such frequency that we were seeing improvement on an almost daily basis, and so we were achieving flow. Workouts got easier, we felt more skilled, and we got faster in the pool, on the bike, and on our runs. And with each moment of progress, we were more "into it."

Give some thought to the creative tension model that we explored in shortcut 4. Analyze your current reality and set a goal.

Turn that goal into a vision. Then develop a step-by-step plan and realistic expectations of the time, energy, and effort required to achieve each step of the plan. Once you've done this, you might decide that achieving the goal isn't worth what it will take to make it happen. That's fine. If you find yourself in this position, immediately identify a new goal. As you consider each step toward the goal, consider the components of creating flow: Does the step present a challenge just beyond your current (or envisioned) skills, knowledge, or performance? Is there a clear goal that will immediately provide feedback on your success? If you can create a state of flow, of optimal experience, you will be much more likely to keep pushing forward.

Recall that I discussed the importance of looking for connections in shortcut 2. The same principle applies here. As you develop your plan, think about moments in the past when you've achieved flow, when you've been successful. If you keep a journal, this is a prime opportunity to look back through it and analyze thoughts and actions around key successes. Develop a plan that is true to you, that leverages the types of steps you need to take or the types of progress points that are meaningful to you to help you attain greater and greater success.

Start small and build confidence. But start! Just starting, just making that decision to do something, will differentiate you from many of your peers who every day avoid making that decision. And having a step-by-step plan makes the prospect of striking out less scary because you can envision the path to success. You just need to leverage self-discipline and focused effort to move you through those steps. And each one will be a win or a learning experience that boosts your confidence.

Along the way, arm yourself with tools that will ensure your success.

Look for Tools to Help

Jane McGonigal is an inspired visionary. If you are a gamer, you know who she is. If not, just watch her TEDx talk or read *Reality Is Broken* to get a sense for her passion for solving the world's problems—through online gaming. As she states boldly on her website, her big goal in life "is to see a game designer nominated for a Nobel Peace Prize." Yep. That's a big goal.

Jane has been earning accolades for years. She was named one of the top thirty-five innovators changing the world through technology in 2006 by MIT's *Technology Review*. In 2008, she had one of the top twenty breakthrough ideas of the year according to *Harvard Business Review*. These are two of many. She was certainly developing competence and building confidence.

And then she hit a hurdle that could have torn that confidence apart. In 2009, she suffered a traumatic brain injury that left her with a concussion. She had headaches, vertigo, memory loss. She couldn't think clearly, and she couldn't work. And because her injury wasn't healing, she became severely depressed and even had thoughts of suicide, which, her doctors told her, were slowing the healing process even more. As she describes it in an Ignite presentation, she made a "last ditch effort to save her quality of life." She created a game to help her recover.

That game—SuperBetter—has been released and is available at www.superbetter.com. It is designed to help people recover from illness and injury but also to help them reach goals that are challenging but positive, goals that may come with mental and emotional hurdles. She calls these goals "epic wins." The amazing thing about the game is that it helps people do exactly what I described above: establish a series of goals, called quests, that keep you on the path to achieving your epic win. You invite allies to help you—friends and family. They can recommend quests for you. Essentially, you are building a community of coaches and supporters. You also identify your "bad guys," which are the things that could keep you from achieving your epic win. The quests are designed to help you defeat your bad guys. To me, this is an ideal tool for helping almost anybody establish a series of wins, step-by-step, and earn an "I can do anything" attitude.

While online gaming may not be for you, it is important to consider the tools that could make achieving your next goal easier. Many avenues are available to find support that will help you achieve goals small and large. That is exactly why I wrote this book. I believe each shortcut, each behavior discussed, is a tool that can increase your odds of success in almost any situation, but especially in your work life.

Many of the shortcuts have an underlying theme of working well with others. Anytime you add people—coworkers, managers, professors, and so on—to the mix, you have added a big variable that can impact your chances of success, either positively or negatively. If you are good with people, you may achieve a goal before you even thought it possible. If you have developed objectionable personality traits, it may take an eternity to meet your goal, especially if you work in a corporate setting. Interpersonal skills are an essential tool that you can leverage.

In shortcut 10, I discuss the importance of having a set of mentors or guides for the journey, something that may be possible only if you can encourage people to support you. What they offer is knowledge and coaching. When Jenny and I were preparing for the Ironman, we befriended more experienced triathletes who became our coaches—overseeing our workouts and training regimen. Their guidance and nutritional advice were key tools that, along with a good bike and running shoes, enabled our Ironman success.

But one of the most entertaining stories I ever heard about the power of a coach came from Joshua Foer, author of *Moonwalking with Einstein*. In an article in the *New York Times Magazine*, Joshua described how, in one year, he went from reporting on the USA Memory Championships to setting the American record for correctly memorizing the order of playing cards in two decks. He did it in 1 minute, 40 seconds. When he originally interviewed competitors, he expected to hear that they were savants with eidetic memories, that they could just look at the cards and remember them. Much to his surprise they all said that they possessed no special talent, no enhanced memory. Instead, they all followed memorization techniques invented in ancient Greece.

Joshua was intrigued. And so began a yearlong journey of research and daily practice. You might think it took hours a day. Nope. He practiced only ten to fifteen minutes a day for about a year. That is all it took for him to progress to the top echelon of U.S. competitors. But he had two tools that he leveraged to make it happen: a coach and knowledge.

After doing some research, he found a professor who confirmed that anyone could learn the classic memorization technique and agreed to coach him. It turns out that the mind remembers pictures better than letters or numbers. And the more silly or outrageous the image, the better we remember it. Here's an example of how Joshua utilized bizarre images to memorize the first five cards in a deck: "Dom DeLuise, the comedian (and five of clubs), was implicated in the following unseemly acts in my mind's eye: He hocked a fat globule of spittle (nine of clubs) on Albert Einstein's thick white mane (three of diamonds) and delivered a devastating karate kick (five of spades) to the groin of

Pope Benedict XVI (six of diamonds)."[5] Joshua went on through the remainder of the 104 cards, using equally vivid images to fix the order in his mind.

We can do some serious learning from this light-hearted anecdote. People who achieve amazing things look like geniuses or savants from the public's vantage point. We believe that no normal person could do what they do. Wrong. When you look behind the curtain, what you inevitably see is that extraordinary achievement is based on leveraging a coach's knowledge to acquire the right tools for the job and having the motivation to put in the hours to meet a series of ever escalating performance goals.

Big Goals Require Big Commitment

When Jenny and I were preparing for the Ironman, we trained fifteen to twenty hours per week for about eighteen months. We were both engineers at Hewlett-Packard at the time and worked about fifty hours a week. During that time, we worked, trained, ate, and slept. The rigors of training led to another important lesson for us: When you choose a time-consuming goal, you're forced to eliminate many of the other things you might want to do. And you need to be highly motivated to make that trade-off.

Now, completing an Ironman might not be your thing. But I believe that everybody has a desire, a dream, a goal to fulfill that motivates them enough to make the necessary sacrifices. The bigger the goal, the bigger the commitment necessary to make it happen. So when you are establishing your goals, make sure that they

---

5. Joshua Foer, "Secrets of a Mind-Gamer," *New York Times Magazine*, February 20, 2011.

are so exciting that the juice you get just from contemplating them fuels your efforts through each step.

Sometimes, commitment also comes with risk. The bigger the goal, the bigger the risks you might have to take to achieve it. But that is an essential building block of the entrepreneurial spirit. And each time you take a risk and succeed, you'll feel more prepared to do it again, more confident that you'll survive what comes. Regardless, if the motivation behind the goal isn't strong enough, your commitment and willingness to take risks to achieve it won't be great enough to see you through.

HP had an in-house class that all managers had to take on the corrective process for poorly performing individuals. The most valuable part of the class advised us, as managers, to figure out whether we were dealing with an ability or a motivation problem. In other words, was the person unable to perform a task or was he not motivated to do it properly or on time? In my experience, not meeting goals is much more likely to be due to a lack of motivation than a lack of ability. A good manager will provide what it takes to help a motivated employee succeed (time and training, generally) but can't run fast enough from an unmotivated or lackluster employee. If you aren't motivated at what you are doing right now as a student or employee, find a new job or course of study immediately. And you might want to reread shortcut 1.

Raw intelligence might be the more important factor if you were required, each day, to do only things that you had never done before and were unlike anything you had ever experienced. But few situations or environments in life are like that. Instead, you need to be motivated enough to do the hard work of making gradual progress and building off each success and failure to become better than others at the tasks required by your chosen path.

When you can make that kind of commitment confidently, you'll understand that you really can do anything.

You will know you have earned an "I can do anything" attitude when something catastrophic happens at work or in life, and instead of panicking, you pause, smile, and say, "Something really good is going to come out of this" or, "This is why they pay us the big bucks (or should)." You'll know when you have mastered this shortcut, and the people around you will, too. Confidence, when it is earned, is easy to recognize, looks good on a person, and is easy to be around. Confidence, when it isn't earned, is arrogance. It looks horrible on a person and is repulsive.

To be honest, and I'm sure you've realized this by now, this shortcut is not much of a shortcut at all. Admittedly, it *is* a lot of work to set a series of goals, to build confidence by meeting them, and over time build an "I can do anything" attitude. But without putting in the work to earn the knowledge that you can achieve anything you commit to, you won't achieve what you are capable of. You won't develop the confidence to aim as high as you should aim, and you won't develop the skills required to hit what you aim for. It's a shortcut to prosperity because, without it, prosperity will always elude you.

Finding the Shortcut

- Are you motivated to work hard enough to earn an "I can do anything" attitude, particularly related to a specific goal or vision? If not, go back to your Prosperity Cycle and examine your motivation. Remember, it comes from a searing hardship you want to overcome or a personal vision so exciting that you can't wait to get to work on making it a reality.

- You will have to fall on your face a couple of times to get to where you want to go, but your face hurts less than you thought it would. Anyone can develop into a person who takes risks, usually succeeding but undaunted after a failure. Are you giving yourself permission to fail? Are you willing to ignore what other people think?

Do Something

- Achieve something that has always eluded you. If you are chronically late, set a goal to go a week without being late to anything. Want to lose five pounds? Set a goal to lose one pound a week for the next five weeks. Obviously, just setting the goal is not enough. You have to do some research and commit to doing the things that will get you there. Perhaps you should set a goal for calories consumed per day and exercise. Earn a success!

- Don't be afraid to ask your boss for direction. Ask her what skills and behaviors she needs most from someone in your position and then work to give it to her. You would be amazed how just asking will separate you from your peers. If you can follow up with real improvement, you will be singled out on performance reviews and talked about at the next level. And, oh yeah, you will get the highest raise and the earliest promotion.

SHORTCUT 7: Recognize and Quickly Analyze Opportunities

One brisk day on the side of a mountain, Rick Alden found himself sitting on a ski lift listening to a Grateful Dead tune. Then his phone rang. Gliding up the hill forty feet above the snow with gloves on, he had to figure out how to unplug his headphones from his iPod and answer a phone that was a zipper and two layers of clothing away. What a pain in the butt.

When Rick couldn't find an existing solution that would make it easier for him to combine sports with his tunes and cell phone, he decided to develop a headphone product of his own. Using his family savings, he hired a contractor to make a prototype. Taking out a loan against the equity in his house, he covered the costs of the first round of inventory. Amazingly, according to an article in *Entrepreneur* magazine, when he talked with his wife about his plan to invest their life savings, she said, "Listen, the worst thing that could possibly happen is the business fails, and we start all over again. That's just not that bad."[6] But the business didn't fail. Rick's initial inventory sold immediately, allowing him to earn a line of credit and fueling the growth of a company that sells incredibly cool, functional headphones and earbuds for snowboarders, skateboarders, and other radical sport enthusiasts.

That company is Skullcandy. In six years, Rick built it from nothing to $100 million in sales. Zero to $100 million in *six years*. Pretty damn impressive.

Rick chose that moment of inconvenience on the chairlift to recognize an opportunity that was waiting to be found. Many people would have passed it by. But prosperous people know that the fastest path to prosperity is to recognize that we are surrounded by opportunities all the time. All we have to do is find a way to get in their path, recognize them when they are in front of us, and then do the legwork to choose the best ones to pursue.

For the most successful entrepreneurs, this is the very core of their worldview. For the rest of us, learning to see and analyze the opportunities that surround us—learning to spot them and quickly assess them by estimating the potential risks and returns in real time—is a habit we can build. I call this becoming an entrepreneurial actuary.

Stop Thinking Like an Employee

While I think being an entrepreneur is awesome, I know it's not for everybody. But being an entrepreneurial actuary is not all about entrepreneurship. Intrapreneurs use the same skills; they just do it from within an established organization. All that matters is that you learn to be aware of those moments when an opportunity

---

6. Jennifer Wang, "*Entrepreneur* Magazine's Entrepreneur of 2009 Award Winners," *Entrepreneur*, December 16, 2009.

presents itself (the essence of entrepreneurship) and learn how to quickly sort out the risks and rewards of pursuing the opportunity (the function of an actuary).

The problem is, we are not typically trained to do this. Our education system works best when students pay attention and avoid distractions. Focus on the work in front of you and accept the solution you're offered. How many times were you encouraged to think of a problem in a different light or to develop your own solution in high school? Probably not often. Early education is there to give you the tools you need to gain perspective, communicate, reason, and solve problems that you are likely to encounter in life. The problem is that the same "color inside the lines" system is employed in most colleges and virtually every workplace that I have ever experienced.

Employers value productivity in the workforce, especially from employees at the entry level. And productivity comes from doing the same activity, the same "right" way every time, getting faster and more proficient each time you do it. The result is to drive quality and productivity up, but the unintended consequence is to deemphasize the use of your brain to figure out better ways to do things. No ad-libbing, please. That's how mistakes are made.

That is also how brilliant revelations occur. In fact, creative thinking was listed as one of the seventeen foundational skills of the twenty-first-century worker by government commissions studying workforce challenges in the United States. If you want to find a shortcut to prosperity, you have to reject the standard dogma that has possibly made you blind to opportunity.

This might seem contradictory to what I encouraged in shortcut 5—learning from the best through education and organizations—but it isn't. You should absolutely go to college. You should absolutely work for great companies. They have amazing foundational knowledge to share—knowledge that you must have before you can start innovating. Highly successful entrepreneurs who dropped out are fun to highlight but are actually the exception to the rule. According to an article by Martin Zwilling, founder of Startup Professionals,

> The most successful entrepreneurs are those with multiple real-life experiences, who have personal exposure to markets where opportunities are being left on the table. Academic research supports that this experience pays off. It also shows that survival prospects are higher if the owner has at least four years of college.[7]

Go to school and work for great companies. But don't let them dull your ability to think creatively. Use your deep knowledge to solve problems differently (better!) than they have been. Because prosperity follows the better idea.

An entrepreneur who follows the "me too" approach as a foundation for a company is asking for trouble. Existing companies with the same solution are much further down the learning curve and have a huge advantage over their newer competitors. Entrepreneurial companies built on a better idea (new solution) have more margin for error. A new product could have a quality problem, long development times, or a big price tag, but if no alternatives exist, customers will purchase them anyway. This buys the entrepreneurs the time to fix their problems as they learn.

Outside of the entrepreneurial realm, smartly managed companies reward employees who consistently come up with new and better ideas and have the ability to lead their implementation. The

---

7. Martin Zwilling, "Most Great Entrepreneurs Don't Drop Out of Harvard," *Fortune*, December 6, 2011.

standardized system referenced earlier makes employees inter-changeable and expendable. Today's worker has very little protection from downturns and mergers. Embrace new ways of doing things, especially when you can prove they are better, and you will add value, prove your worth, and differentiate yourself.

The most successful entrepreneurs in the world are rule breakers who think that the rules were invented for others, not them. Have you ever wanted to try on that attitude? Now's the time. In almost every picture I have seen of Rick Alden, Skullcandy's logo—a human skull—is splashed across the front of his T-shirt, and his expression is a cross between a self-satisfied smirk and contempt for anyone who values conformity. If you think you want to go down the entrepreneur route or even if you want to pursue your interests in another way, you are going to have to adopt a little of Rick's attitude and let your internal rebel out of its cage once in a while. You will find that it is a lot easier to spot and analyze opportunities without the blindfold created by years of conformity.

John Torrens, professor of entrepreneurship at Syracuse University, helped explain this to me by offering up his favorite definition of entrepreneurship: "The pursuit of an opportunity without regard to resources under control." He explained that entrepreneurs choose not to see limiters such as prohibitive rules or critical resources that they may not have access to. Instead they simply identify an opportunity and envision the best alternative to capitalize on the opportunity and then figure out how to make it possible.

What do these opportunities offer to your individual prosperity other than the potential for career growth? The catalyst for the next iteration of the Prosperity Cycle. Each opportunity you face requires a decision to do something, a decision to start in on the cycle again with a different point of focus and a different end goal. The more opportunities you pursue, the more iterations of the Prosperity Cycle you will experience, and the faster you will move toward your vision.

Hunting Opportunities

Great opportunities come in two kinds: random and precipitated. Random opportunities are happenstance—situations you walk into through sheer luck. Of course, being fortunate is only half the battle. You also need to be aware that an opportunity has just presented itself and then develop a plan to exploit it. The other kind of opportunity is one that is precipitated by your own actions. By interacting with the normal players in your life (friends, associates, bosses, etc.) you can create an opportunity that wouldn't likely occur.

Ken Salazar's biggest advantage in life was his mom and dad's belief system. He was raised to have an "I can do anything" attitude. His father, a first-generation American of Mexican descent, worked his way through dental school and established a successful practice, so understood the power of hard work, and his mom was convinced that her eldest son would be the CEO of a big company.

And yet Ken struggled in his freshman year of college, enjoying his newfound freedom and losing his scholarship when he failed to attain the required GPA. Even worse than losing his scholarship, Ken felt he had disappointed his father. After vowing that he would never do it again, he proceeded to turn things around by deciding to make the most of every opportunity that came his way. Ken was in his junior year as a business major at Arizona State when he interviewed with PricewaterhouseCoopers, the big four accounting firm, for an internship. He didn't hear back from them. For most people, that would be the end of the story. But not for

Ken. He did some research and found that PwC's internship program was handled by an HR manager in the Los Angeles office.
Ken called him and was told that all the internship positions had
been filled. Still, that wasn't the end of the story. Ken somehow
managed to convince the manager to assign him to a new internship that had recently been approved.

Impressive, right? Yes, but there's more. After reporting to
work at the PwC LA office, Ken was assigned to the dispute analysis department, the group charged with collecting data in support
of the client's position in disputed claims. It took only a couple
of weeks for Ken to conclude that this was really boring work
and that the guys in the business recovery systems (BRS) division, which helped turn around troubled companies, were having
a lot more fun and making a lot more money. You could tell, he
said, because their partner offices were bigger. So after stumbling
across an e-mail distribution list for everyone in the BRS division,
Ken decided it would be a great idea for him to draft a witty and
compelling mass e-mail to let everyone there know that he would
prefer to work for them. In the e-mail, he referred to himself as a
"dehydrated sponge" ready to soak up all there was to learn and
clean up any mess. Ken had just hit "send" and sat back in his
chair, satisfied with his e-mail masterpiece, when his phone rang
and he was summoned to the HR manager's office. Ken skipped
down the hall, thinking, "They must really want me!"

When he got to the manager's office, he wasn't so sure. "That
was pretty bold," the guy said, and not in an admiring way. But
Ken, the kid from Albuquerque, knew that sometimes you have to
make your own opportunities. And in the end he was proved right.
The HR manager admitted that he had received several calls from
managers in the BRS division asking that Ken be reassigned to their
team. A new intern who had the *cojones* to send a division-wide

e-mail and offer to clean up any mess they could throw at him sounded a lot better than the timid, brain-dead interns they were used to working with.

Ken is one of the nicest, most respectful rebels you will ever meet, but a rebel nonetheless. But why did his strategy work? Because he ignored the status quo while offering to add value.

Create Opportunity by Adding Value in Every Interaction

Most of us go through life looking for people to help us solve our problems. At the same time, lots of us also go through life trying to avoid getting entangled in other people's problems. If you are one of those rare people who, with great sincerity, offer to help—to add value—incredible opportunities will present themselves.

I was an engineer with a couple of years' experience at HP when I ran into a classic feud that occurs between engineers and production on the shop floor. Engineers like to tell production how to improve their processes, and production personnel like to tell the engineers that they don't know what they're talking about. I don't even remember what the argument was about, but I pissed off the production manager—enough that he went up the ladder and complained to his boss. A turf battle ensued and I got a heads-up that the manufacturing manager was about to contact my boss's boss (two levels up from me) about the situation. Crap.

After an hour or so of worrying, I decided to beat them to the punch and inform my boss's boss, a man whom I had had virtually no direct contact with and who didn't know me from Adam. I walked into his office, introduced myself, and let him know that he was about to get a call from the manufacturing manager about me. Without giving him much background on the issue or defending my position, I simply told him that he was paying me way too much money to have to deal with petty stuff like this and that I would resolve the problem to everyone's satisfaction by the end of the day. And through a combination of problem solving and groveling, I did exactly that.

It might not seem that I had added value or solved a problem, because I had created the problem to begin with. But I could have walked into his office on the defensive, ranting about production and taking a hard position. By promising to resolve the conflict, I kept him out of it. I had brought him a problem, but I had also delivered a solution—something you should always do, especially with a boss. I never talked to him again other than to say hello in the hall, but a few months later I realized this one interaction might have been a game changer for me. I was awarded a company-paid scholarship (salary plus tuition) to attend Stanford to earn a master's degree. And after completing the degree, I found myself on the fast track for the remaining five years that I spent at HP.

People love to talk about their problems and their successes. Careful and skilled listening, however, is a more crucial skill in adding value and generating opportunities. Many entrepreneurs don't have the patience for it, but those who do discover the power to access vast opportunities. Listening and communicating well are also critical to adding value in a team environment. Anything worth achieving is going to require a team, and adding value to a team means listening and relating to those around you in a way that makes sense to them. These types of interactions cause people to be attracted to you and your cause. Attracting the best and brightest to your team is one of the most effective shortcuts to prosperity that I know of.

Become a "can do" problem solver and listen carefully to

those around you to add value in your interactions. People avoid the whiner and gravitate toward (and promote or support) the person who has never seen a problem that couldn't be solved.

Learn to Spot Opportunities

Anytime you find yourself saying, "Wow!" or "Holy crap!" or "Cool!" or "Huh?" and especially, "Someone ought to figure out how to . . ." you can bet that you've just encountered the source of an opportunity. Let me give you some examples.

Landing in London, I watched a friend pop a local SIM card into his unlocked cell phone so that he could pay a few cents per minute to place calls instead of the $1.50 per minute I would be paying. *Cool*, I thought. And then, *I wonder what kind of online fulfillment business I could start that would prepare cell phone users for international trips?* Ken Grunski wondered the same thing and founded Telestial, a successful telecommunications company that offers prepaid SIM cards that work in 180 countries.

Several years ago I noticed an increasing number of older people suffering from respiratory problems that required them to be tethered to an oxygen tank. Shortly after that, I saw a guy playing golf with a lightweight liquid oxygen system clipped to his belt. *Wow.* And then, *How much would someone with COPD (13 million diagnosed in the United States) pay to get their life back?* My wife, Jenny, created the Oxygen Concentrator Store, a web-based company that has sold thousands of portable oxygen concentrators to customers who are happy to be free from the hassle of dealing with oxygen tanks.

How do you train yourself to notice opportunities like these or opportunities within an organization? Here are a few tips.

Get a job in sales. Nothing accelerates opportunity recognition faster than a job in sales. Every successful salesperson excels at adding value and assessing opportunities. We all like to buy from upbeat, engaging salespeople who listen well enough to understand our unique problems, propose sensible solutions, and come across as absolutely committed to the product or service that they are promoting. Sound familiar?

If you can't stand the idea of sales, you might try keeping an idea list. Create a recurring appointment on your calendar and spend a few minutes at the end of each day rewinding your day and recalling any time you were inconvenienced, experienced something that you thought was cool, or found yourself saying that "someone should figure out how to . . ." Then quickly brainstorm a few ideas for how to address these opportunities. Try this daily for a month, which is typically the amount of time it takes to develop a habit. After a month, I bet you'll be spotting opportunities on a daily basis.

Business models and value chains are a great source of opportunity inspiration. If you are employed, your employer has established a business model that more than justifies your salary. Take the time to understand that business model and you'll start seeing opportunities within the value chain and ways to develop an even better model if you want to strike out on your own.

Once you start seeing them, you'll be amazed at how many there are. Then all you have to decide is which ones are worth pursuing.

Calculating the Odds

Just because you have a great idea doesn't mean that it is viable, either financially or in other ways, or that it is the right opportunity for you. Even successful entrepreneurs kiss a lot of frogs before they find their prince, but it's better if you can analyze opportunities to minimize your missteps. Quickly analyzing and sorting ideas by their potential is a huge shortcut to prosperity, and it's easy to do.

I introduced you to Steve Goldman back in shortcut 5. Before he and his partner founded Workforce Insight, their workforce management software and services company, Steve evaluated dozens of other potential business ideas. I got a kick out of one in particular. During a business trip to Las Vegas, Steve and his partner had an aha moment when they realized that there must be a way to capitalize on all of the business people who attend conferences in Vegas only to find that they drank a little too much the night before and need help recovering. They envisioned a company where all known hangover cures could be found under one roof. In addition to over-the-counter remedies, the concept encompassed staffing the company with a medical doctor who could address dehydration and other side effects by utilizing IVs, oxygen, and physician-monitored procedures designed to get someone back in the game (pun intended) quickly.

Before we dismiss Steve's idea as frivolous, let's take a few minutes to do a quick and dirty economic analysis of it. Get ready, because the numbers and the assumptions are gonna start flying. Our challenge is to use common sense to come up with estimates of market size and cost to deduce potential revenue and profit. A good place to start would be to estimate the number of people who visit Las Vegas annually. I don't know that number, but I do know that most will stay in a hotel. I also know that Las Vegas is one of the biggest hotel markets in the United States, so I take a guess and estimate Vegas to have 100,000 hotel rooms. (Google confirmed that there are 125,000 hotel rooms in Vegas when I checked, but let's go with my number for simplicity.) I then further assume that all visitors are potential customers (not just businessmen), the average stay is two nights, all rooms are rented to a single guest, and the hotels all average 50 percent occupancy for the year. With those assumptions, I can calculate that the annual number of potential customers for this service is 9,125,000 (100,000 × .50 × [365/2]). If I further assume that only 5 percent of them will drink too much (pretty conservative, if my last trip to Vegas was any indication) and that I can figure out how to convince 5 percent of that 5 percent to become clients, a hangover recovery center would have a potential customer base of about 22,800 people a year (9,125,000 × .05 × .05). That's not bad.

But how does it look financially? In order to keep things simple, we can capture the majority of the costs by estimating the cost of the facility, physicians, staff, and overhead. I would imagine that space on the strip is pricey. I quickly found some near the strip for $30 per square foot, and I'm betting that on-strip space might run twice that cost. If we could find a small space for lease, we could probably make do with one thousand square feet. That would be $60,000 a year in rent. A quick search told me that a general physician makes about $150,000 a year and we would need two of them to provide coverage every day of the week. Additional staff (say four employees, including a nurse and a receptionist for each doc) cost another $200,000 or so. And other overhead might run the company, say, $15,000 per month in phone, utilities, medical supplies, etc., so another $180,000 per year. That brings us to a rough total of $740,000 a year to run the company. You would obviously need an initial investment in furniture and equipment, but we can come back and estimate start-up capital requirements if our profitability estimates look good.

What do I think people would be willing to pay to get back an entire day in Vegas, particularly if they've got only two days to enjoy themselves? A conservative estimate might be $75, which would bring in revenue of $1,710,000. So, before taxes, we would be left with $970,000 or 57 percent in pretax profit, assuming our estimates are in the ballpark.

Interesting. This might be a viable idea. Except of course for all of the variables we haven't taken into consideration and all of the assumptions we made. For example if we attract only 2 percent of hangover victims instead of 5 percent we swing from a sizable profit to losing money. It is important to remember that this is just a ballpark estimate of the economic value of the idea. If I liked the concept and lived in Vegas, I might take the time to do the research necessary to develop a real business plan and confirm the assumptions. I would have to research how medical clinics operate, get real numbers to replace all of my estimates, think about how much I have to invest to get started, and consider the potential risks. What if the hotels catch on and create an in-room concierge service? What if people aren't willing to spend more than $30 on a hangover cure? How much will insurance cost? On the other hand, what if I can partner with an innovative hotel that would be willing to provide space at no cost and make referrals from the hotel concierge?

Hmm. It might be worth it. Or it might not be worth the risk. If I were really passionate about it, I'd just have to do more research to find out.

This approach to assessing an opportunity financially is great for entrepreneurial ideas, but it works just as well for a process improvement idea (how much time would be saved and therefore how much money?) that an enterprising employee might propose. You could also use this approach to analyze a career move (what would my new salary be and how would my long-term earning potential change compared to the cost of living in a more expensive city?). And at any company, if you show leadership that you have thought through the financial implications of your ideas, you'll be a rock star, because few "employee minded" people do.

But Is It a Fit for You?

Any time we are considering an opportunity, more is at stake than money. You have to ask, "Is this the right opportunity *for me?*" Meandering through life leaping at one opportunity after another without any sense of where you're headed is not the best way to achieve what you want. You may get there eventually, but it will probably be a very roundabout path.

Understanding who you are and developing your personal vision are great starting points for assessing how an opportunity fits you on a personal level. The list shown here explains how to leverage those pieces of knowledge to assess whether an opportunity is fundamentally attractive to you.

Attributes of Attractive Opportunities

Differentiation: Whether you are looking at a new job or starting a new company, does the opportunity allow you to differentiate yourself through your knowledge, skills, talents, passions, or other attributes?

Scalability: Can it lead to dramatic growth? With respect to an offer of employment, is it likely to lead to greater opportunity in the future? A high-paying job with no opportunity for advancement or learning isn't as appealing as a lower-paying job that puts you on a path of career growth. If it's an idea for a new business or a new product or service to add in your company, how much growth can you expect from it in the future, not just the first year?

Barriers to entry: How hard is it for competitors to take advantage of the same opportunity? Do you have special knowledge, skills, or talents that allow you to exploit this opportunity more successfully than others?

Minimal risk: For offers of employment, look for the stability of the company behind the offer and the opportunity for growth and advancement. To minimize the risk of a start-up, look for opportunities that:

- You can pursue while retaining your day job.
- Require a minimum of start-up capital.
- Are resistant to an economic downturn or changing consumer preference (fads).

Use this list to play with any opportunity that comes your way. If it fails in more than one of these, you should probably pass or think of ways to modify it to make it work. You can also download a tool from www.shortcuttoprosperity.com to help you assess opportunities for their risks and returns and their fit with your goals.

When I spoke with Mike Aviles, he described a very similar approach to how he began selecting CEO opportunities after the first company he led was sold. He wanted to be strategic, and so he decided to take a sabbatical and select his next move carefully. He knew that his next job had to be right for his family, had to offer a lot of money, and had to offer the ability to learn and gain professional cred, which probably meant changing industries. This was all happening in 1998 and 1999, when the market was hot. "Opportunities were coming at me left and right. Over a period of about a year, I had about thirty-three CEO opportunities come my way. Of the thirty-three, I looked at twelve of them hard. Of the twelve, I got offered eight. I turned down seven of them over about six or seven months before taking the eighth one. People would say to me, 'For an unemployed guy, you sure are picky.' But I knew exactly what I wanted, and I was confident enough, patient enough, and willing to work hard enough to go find it."

Depending on the economy or your industry or where you are in your career, you may not be able to be as picky with your opportunities as Mike was, but that doesn't mean you shouldn't be very strategic about choosing the opportunities you pursue. If you leap at the first thing that comes your way, you aren't employing the principles of personal entrepreneurship, and you are inviting the winds of change to push you in whatever direction they like. And even more problematic is the fact that you are launching a new trip around the Prosperity Cycle that you aren't likely to finish, wasting effort and energy. Ask yourself, are you prepared to do the legwork and the strategic analysis to find the right opportunity for you?

Opportunities abound. Today you will be in the presence of opportunities, and they will pass you by. I guarantee it. That's fine if they are opportunities you aren't interested in. It's lousy if they have the potential to change your life for the better.

Learn to be aware of the multitude of opportunities that pass by you daily. Successful entrepreneurs and intrapreneurs have trained themselves to see them, evaluate them, and categorize them. And they think about doing it about as much as they think about breathing. The best of the best have expanded their "grasp" to include any opportunity that they can imagine a path to. They aren't deterred by convention, social norms, organizational charts, or financial constraints. If you are serious about being more prosperous, get ready to get out of your comfort zone.

In the next part of the book, we'll explore how to build a team around you that will help you take advantage of the opportunities you decide to pursue. Your odds of success go up considerably when you have smart people with you in the trenches and trusted advisers telling you how they succeeded at what you are trying to do.

Finding the Shortcut

- Everyone has a unique perspective from which to view the world we live in. Your personal vantage point allows you to see opportunities differently than anyone else. Believe this and you will start to see and appreciate opportunities that you didn't notice before.

- Thoughtful individuals have drawn conclusions based on a lifetime of data, and you have a lot to learn from their insight. If it's worth your time to listen to someone in the first place, find ways to add value to the conversation. Ask probing questions. Look for ways to help advance their thinking and see where it leads.

Do Something

- Keep an idea journal for a week or two, writing down potential business ideas that occur to you. Take the most intriguing idea and sketch out a business model leveraging the insight. Do a five-minute financial analysis to evaluate its commercial viability and decide whether it warrants more detailed study.
- Pick a day and concentrate on adding value to every interaction that you are a part of during that day. Write a symbol on your hand or wear an old watch to subtly remind yourself of the exercise. Watch the energy change when you actively listen and focus exclusively on attaining whatever it is that the other party is interested in. Watch opportunities flow your way. You can always say no.

Recruit Allies

SHORTCUT 8: Genuinely Care About Other People

Dale Carnegie is the guru of interpersonal skills. In one of the best-selling books of all time, *How to Win Friends and Influence People* (more than 15 million copies sold since it was first published in 1937), he outlines strategies to help you do just that. Are his ideas complex and difficult to implement? No. Smile, listen, develop a genuine interest in others, make them feel important, give honest and sincere appreciation. Beneath all of the pragmatism runs an important and humanist refrain: Be sincere, be authentic, be genuine, and show people that you care.

Why am I talking about this in a book about achieving personal prosperity? Why does this matter when I've said that achieving prosperity usually means breaking away from the pack and going out on your own? Even when you are pursuing your own personal vision, even when you are trying to differentiate yourself, you'll find that other people's paths overlap with yours. Few things worth doing can be done by an individual alone. They are achieved by focused and highly motivated groups of people.

You need those people. When your path overlaps with others', show them that you care enough to help them in their pursuits. Caring leads to trust, and when they trust you, they'll turn around and help you right back.

Caring → Trust → Prosperity

Leaders of the most successful organizations are creating cultures of caring, and they don't see any irony in the fact that empathy is the key to their market domination. It keeps them nimble, it helps them evolve, and it makes them capable and productive. Caring is the key to their prosperity, because they need people on their side who want to see them succeed.

Likewise, very few personal visions of prosperity can be achieved without interacting synergistically with a whole bunch of people—teammates, friends, customers, suppliers, partners, investors, mentors. It's simply not possible to acquire all of the skills and knowledge and connections you need on your own. While the initial decision to start a new Prosperity Cycle may be entirely yours, the moment you make that decision, you will need people in your life who have your back, as many as you can get. How you interact with them can either put your dream on the fast track or guarantee that it will never happen. Who will help you sustain the energy to move forward? Who will hold you accountable for meeting goals? Who will encourage you to see the learning potential in those moments when you fall short? You need people you can trust.

Trust. It's a rare commodity in life, especially in business. The days of doing business on a handshake are gone. Contracts are ten times longer than they used to be. But legalese can't fix a flawed relationship. We all understand this implicitly, and so people and organizations gravitate toward those of us who have proven that we are trustworthy—we will do what we say we are going to do, we don't have hidden agendas, and we care about others' success as well as our own.

Think about somebody you know whom you just can't trust. He or she may not have done anything particularly awful, but the trust isn't there. We all know these people. We tolerate them. We don't go out of our way to make them enemies, but we certainly don't go out of our way to help them. Now think about all of the people you know whom you would use as personal references. You know they would say only positive things. In fact, they mostly say positive things about everybody they meet. And they mean it. They go out of their way to help and to encourage others. They are prosperous and generous.

Build your personal brand on this foundation. Organizations recognize people who get things done, and being trusted makes you incredibly productive. People who learn the skills of caring and building trust will become leaders. And their teams will be the ones making incredible things happen. Why? Because caring and building trust are surefire, pragmatic techniques for making everything go faster. Stephen M.R. Covey, author of *The Speed of Trust*, wrote of trust, "If developed and leveraged, that one thing has the potential to create unparalleled success and prosperity in every dimension of life." He used communication to explain how trust increases speed and productivity: "In a high-trust relationship, you can say the wrong thing, and people will still get your meaning. In a low-trust relationship, you can be very measured, even precise, and they'll still misinterpret you."[8] If you can't build trust with the people you need to work with, you should expect progress to be painstakingly slow.

True prosperity means having fun, and it is incredibly difficult to have fun all by yourself. Prosperity requires relationships, and those relationships have to be a part of your vision. It is highly improbable that your vision of prosperity is you alone on a mountaintop for the next thirty years. You also need to be happy with who you are, and people who treat others poorly or simply don't care are not likely to be proud of their behavior—unless of course they are psychopaths. Caring about others, helping them in their own quest, will make you feel super about where you are and how you got there.

Care and model the behaviors that lead to trust, and people will beat a path to your path—they will help you on your journey. Your probability of success will skyrocket. Fail to care and you will never achieve real prosperity.

Getting Pragmatic

If people know you care about them, it follows that you have their best interests at heart. Trust follows naturally from this kind of relationship. How do you prove yourself to others? Here are some tips.

Give Freely

In his fantastic book *Love Is the Killer App*, Tim Sanders writes, "Those of us who use love as a point of differentiation in business

---

8. Stephen M.R. Covey, *The Speed of Trust* (Free Press, 2006), 1, 6.

will separate ourselves from our competitors just as world-class distance runners separate themselves from the rest of the pack trailing behind them."[9] I couldn't agree more. The important thing is to recognize that not everybody is a competitor. Most people in your life can be pulled into your support system, and you should want to be pulled into theirs. Tim's advice is to share your knowledge, your network, and your compassion. What he's saying is, "Add value in any way you can."

You have the opportunity to add value with every person you meet. But you have to care enough to be willing to give, to be generous. To be a truly giving person, you have to develop an abundance mentality. It's hard to hope for the best for others or help them toward their goals if you think that their good fortune comes at your expense. Some games in the world have to be played win–lose, but most relationships aren't defined that way. The people and organizations that are going to speed you toward your personal prosperity certainly shouldn't be viewed through that lens. Growing, thriving organizations raise all boats. Positive relationships with prosperous people do the same. The pie of life has an almost infinite opportunity to grow. It's not a zero-sum game. And you can engineer your own expanding pie. But it will take the help of others. You should be happy to share it with them.

The Power of Pause

We live in a world that operates in small bursts and at the speed of light. Yesterday was a light e-mail day and I received 112 messages. My spam filter automatically snagged 31, I deleted another 51 after reading and processing them, and 30 remain in my in-box today. Your in-box is probably similar. Because of the flood of

9. Tim Sanders, *Love Is the Killer App* (Crown Business, 2002), 11.

information we receive, most of us have e-mail down to a science. Open, skim, and delete or send a quickly composed, cryptic, self-centered response. In fact, this reflects how most of us communicate with others—regardless of medium. And most of us are missing an opportunity. Big-time.

The problem is that we jump from receiving to reacting, without even a moment of pause between the two. That moment presents a world of opportunities, a wonderful place where we can show that we genuinely care about other people. Think about how it feels to read an e-mail that frames an issue from your perspective, that reflects an understanding of your concerns, and proposes an action that is sensible *to you*. It's refreshing! And it is also among the lowest of low-hanging fruit in the quest to communicate that you care. This is what you can achieve when you leverage the power of pause.

Here's how to do it.

> **Step 1: Be a world-class listener.** Whether you are hearing or reading information from a person you care about, focus on it. Take your self-focused lens and turn it around. Read an e-mail completely; don't just read the first sentence and assume you know where it's going. When somebody is talking to you about a subject that is important, don't multitask.
>
> **Step 2: Pause.** Think about the source of the information. What is the issue at hand and how does it look to that person? What is her perspective? What does this person need? How does she prefer to communicate? Unless it's a complete stranger, you can come up with the answers to these questions fairly quickly, usually in a matter of seconds. Integrate what you've heard and what you know with your

own experience. Consider how your insights allow you to add meaning to the subject or help solve a problem.

Step 3: Offer clear, thoughtful ideas and communication in response. Provide a response that gives the person what he needs and shows him that you've listened carefully and care enough to consider the issue from more than one angle, your own. Your response will be more meaningful than most he will receive that day.

Does it take more time to communicate this way? Sure. But, in my experience, you are better off taking the extra ten to fifteen seconds to frame your answer with the recipient in mind, with a goal of adding value, and with the intent of showing that you care.

Even when we develop a habit of communicating in this way, there are moments when our resolve is tested. When someone throws out a verbal zinger, it's hard not to reflexively respond with a defensive and trust-destroying response. I should know; I'm pretty good at it. If I'm not consciously counteracting it, my natural response is to defend against the comment and deflect it in another direction—throwing somebody else under the bus along the way. The power of pause is more important in these interactions than in most others, because this is where trust is tested. During the pause, think of the zinger as a harmless cosmic ray, one of millions that pass through you every second. Take the time to acknowledge what is being said and consider what components you agree with and disagree with. Personal communication is rarely black-and-white.

Your response will be measured and will build trust by reinforcing that you care.

Carefrontation

While I was earning my master's degree at Stanford, I took a trip down the California coast to Yosemite National Park with Jenny. We spent a couple of days hiking, taking in the incredible beauty of the valley. On Sunday morning before we moved on, we attended a service at a nondenominational chapel in the park. In the sermon, the minister shared a concept that I had never heard before but that I would use often from that day forward: "carefrontation."

Just as the word combines caring and confrontation, the minister explained that confronting and caring about somebody at the same time is incredibly powerful. In fact, it's necessary. Confronting someone is inherently a jarring and painful process. To have any hope of helping that person embrace an opportunity to make personal change for the better, he or she had better believe that you truly care. In fact, if they *do* know you care, you can say almost anything without offending them.

Part of the burden of caring for people is that you want to help them do better, you want to help them move their Prosperity Cycles along. A friend of mine, Rick, told me that when he sits down to discuss an issue with a member of his team, he asks for their permission to carefront them. "In the future, if I see that you are doing something self-limiting, do I have your permission to confront you about it?" he asks. That is a powerful approach, because he is essentially entering into a contract with that person. He is committing to care enough to confront the person in order to help them improve. That person, if they agree, is committing to being open to that feedback and understanding its origin—a place of caring.

Rick took this path with a person on his team who had a very negative, gloomy attitude. People avoided him, colleagues did not want to partner with him, and he was not going to progress in the organization. He was an idea killer and had a serious case of Eeyore Syndrome. Through a series of carefrontations, my friend helped that man turn his attitude and perspective around and become a much more valued and liked team member. Of course, he could have ignored the problem and eventually fired the man as his ability to contribute to the team devolved. But that is not what you do when you care about somebody.

Carefrontation also makes sense because, like any other sustainable action, you benefit as much from the action as the person being carefronted. Not only does the team that you are a part of perform better when someone makes a change for the better, it just feels great to help someone become more successful and fulfilled because of your coaching. In a world that often defaults to win–lose, the person whose actions are demonstrative of a win–win philosophy attracts the best opportunities. And win–win leaders attract the best talent and, more often than not, field the winning team.

Leveraging the concept of carefrontation to drive personal and organizational change was more effective than any other leadership skill I learned or witnessed in my twenty-five years in business leadership. But be warned: People have amazingly sensitive bullshit detectors. We can all tell instantly where the motivation for feedback or advice comes from. If it comes from the heart, it slices through someone's carefully constructed layers of defense like a warm knife through butter. Carefrontation only works when the caring is genuine.

Carefrontation is a transformational method of adding value. You can help somebody eliminate a self-limiting behavior. You can help a team change its trajectory by improving how it functions.

Imagine an entire organization full of people who trust each other, care about each other, and provide feedback that causes personal and organizational performance to grow continuously. Leaders who wield carefrontation possess a competitive weapon more powerful than anything money can buy.

Lead for the Benefit of Others

Few of us will develop personal visions that don't require us to take a leadership position somewhere along the way. It may be as a manager in an organization, it may be as an entrepreneur, it may be as the chair of some philanthropic activity. At some point, if you want to be prosperous, you have to step up and lead. When that happens, you become responsible for the success of other people. If you are a leader and don't understand that statement, you need to seriously reconsider your approach. For your team members to succeed, they have to feel that you care for them and they have to trust you. And this is how you will succeed as well.

Genuinely caring about your team members and helping them to grow and achieve their personal visions while teaching them to care about each other is the best way I know to build a high-performing team. Trust through displayed caring drives team performance more potently than any other factor except the strength of the individuals themselves. Here's how:

- Better ideas. Teams that care and trust share their best ideas without worrying about pride of authorship. They give voice to radical ideas without fear of being judged. Good teams tackle problems through productive brainstorming. Want some examples? Read any of the books about IDEO, possibly the most productive and innovative design firm in the world.

- Better synergy. Teams are most effective when they are all pulling together in the same direction. In the absence of suspicion and concerns about self-serving actions, mutual support exists.
- Greater efficiency. Poorly performing teams (without caring and trust) waste a lot of time and energy being counterproductive. They don't share information and certainly don't support each other's efforts. Remember Stephen Covey's points on the speed of trust. When a team has trust, productivity and innovation skyrocket.

As a leader, you can expand the Prosperity Cycle from the individual level to the team level. Team performs well. Team wins. Team celebrates. Team raises its goals and goes bigger. Every individual benefits—including you.

Steve Goldman understands this concept better than anyone I have ever met. He is the thirty-nine-year-old cofounder and CEO of Workforce Insight, whom I first told you about in shortcut 5. He was also the man with the plan to create hangover recovery centers in Las Vegas, which he never pursued. This was a good move, because after starting Workforce Insight five years ago, Steve and his cofounder, Don, have built a rocket ship of a company that is growing at almost 100 percent annually and just passed $20 million in sales.

When I asked Steve how he defined prosperity, he didn't hesitate a beat in saying that, beyond meeting basic needs, prosperity isn't about money as much as it is about how happy you are, how much love you have in your life, and how much learning you are doing. Most people struggle or at least take some time to answer that question. But Steve had an experience that forced him to a point of clarity.

Earlier this year Steve was the first person to come upon a horrific car accident on a sparsely populated rural highway. There had been a head-on collision. One car was upside down and forty feet down an embankment. The other car was still on the roadway but was annihilated. He went to this car first and found a family of five trapped in the vehicle. The father and a fourteen-year-old son in the backseat were already dead. The mother was in the passenger seat, pinned in the wreckage but not seriously hurt. Her nineteen-year-old son and eight-year-old daughter were in the back seat. Both had serious head injuries, but the daughter's was the most critical. Steve, who is the father of two daughters himself, held the unconscious, critically injured girl while emergency vehicles made their way to the accident site. He tried desperately to keep the mother calm while keeping her daughter breathing. The little girl died in the hospital four days later.

Steve described himself as beyond sad for weeks, crying every time his mind took him back to the horror of the accident. He was only able to move on when he realized two things. First, horrific accidents like this happen all the time, and this one was different only because he was there to witness it. And second, he had found an answer to the question, "Why was I there?" He concluded that the experience served to test his strength and help him gain perspective that could change his life. The perspective? Life is short, so he better be doing what he loved and loving those around him.

This may have been a new level of clarity for Steve, but love was certainly not a new concept for him. Before he and Don founded the company, they spent some time at the whiteboard brainstorming what they thought was important. The first bullet on their list was to create a "Place for employees to love / grow / be a real part of."

So how does Steve do this? He sets an example of caring for the whole company to emulate. Here's what I heard from those who work with him:

- Steve is a good listener and perceptive. He asks probing questions and is world class at teasing information out of a conversation without being obtrusive.
- He prides himself on knowing where good work is being done and praising the people responsible.
- Because caring requires paying attention, Steve seems to know the issues and pressures felt by every employee in his company.
- No subject is taboo with Steve. You can ask any question and he will answer it to the best of his ability and without retribution, whether the question is about the company's strategy, financials, compensation, or values.
- Steve wants all of his employees to know what they want and what he can do to help them achieve it. He asks them those questions when they are hired.
- He tells people in the clearest of terms that he cares about them: He tells them that he loves them.

Are you like Steve? If not, take a lesson from his playbook and show your team that you care.

The higher your aspirations, the more people you will need on your team to help you achieve them. Caring enough to provide opportunities for people to pursue their own visions creates win–win situations and builds trust. Do good for others and they'll do good for you.

Finding the Shortcut

- Recruiting allies is enabled by people knowing that you would enjoy seeing them succeed and that you will do whatever you can to help them. You can't fake this, nor should you try. If you are in a leadership position, surround yourself with people you feel this way about. If you aren't yet in a position to build your own team, invest in like-minded peers in preparation for the future. Great teams seem to come together when the time is right.

- Genuinely caring about other people is a great foundation for your personal brand—the characteristics and abilities that you become known for. Think about your current brand and its elements. Is your brand helping you achieve prosperity? If you haven't already read it, pick up Dan Schawbel's *Me 2.0* on building a personal brand. It's a powerful concept.

Do Something

- Look for people you work with who show that they care about others. You can recognize them by the size of their network and the demand for their involvement in key projects. How do they make that happen in your environment? Adopt the behaviors that work for you and start integrating them into your standard interaction style. You'll see your own personal network grow, and you'll become one of those people who just seem to be on the way up.

- Leverage the power of the pause. When communicating in person, practice waiting a fraction of a second before you respond, especially to inflammatory remarks. Frame your answer to ignore negativity and to provide a thoughtful response that incorporates the other person's perspective.

- Try responding to less e-mail, but for each e-mail you do choose to answer, invest the time to put yourself in the sender's shoes and compose a response that reflects that person's unique perspective and needs. People won't notice the e-mail you don't respond to, but your thoughtful responses will be a dramatic differentiator for you.

- Go out of your way once a week to help somebody learn a new skill, progress with a project, or make a connection he or she needs. And then wait for the caring karma to come your way.

SHORTCUT 9: Partner Wisely and Broadly

Without the help of some amazing partners, I wouldn't be where I am today. Not even close. In fact, anybody who tells you that they've achieved great success without building crucial personal and business relationships is lying to you.

Warning: In the next sentences, I'm going to get sappy. The most important partner in my life? My wife, Jenny, hands down. Do you remember the story I told about deciding to leave HP to go to Emerson Electric so that I could gain the skills I needed to start my own company? Well, here's the rest of the story.

This revelation hit me when I was in the process of building a house, and Jenny was expecting our first child. Adding a new job to the list would complete the life change trifecta—three changes you should avoid tackling at the same time. When I found the job at Emerson, it was ideal for my career growth but less than ideal for our family life. I would have to commute two hours a day and be in the office six days a week. Jenny would essentially become a single parent with a demanding job (she was in a management position at HP). She would be on her own, figuring out daycare and pickup times and doctor visits and a host of other challenges.

I had known for some time that I had won the matrimonial lottery when I married Jenny, but when I told her about the job offer, she showed me that I didn't know the half of it. "I've got this," she said. "We both want the same thing, and someone needs to hold down the fort while the other makes it happen. You should go for it."

Six years later, when I started Peak Industries, Jenny came through again—with even more support. In addition to managing the family (we had two kids by then), she upped the ante. She told me not to worry if I didn't bring home what I had earned in the past. Her salary could cover the mortgage and the household expenses of a scaled-back lifestyle. She took away the biggest obstacle between my future vision and my current reality. I'm certain I would not have started Peak Industries if it meant putting my family's well-being at risk.

Every day, I recognize how lucky I am to have Jenny as a partner. Today, we're more than husband and wife; we're also business partners. What Jenny brings to the table is a set of strengths and talents that balance my own along with shared values, an understanding of who I am as a person, honesty, and generosity—I know she has my best interests at heart. I hope that I offer her the same in return, because these are the core elements of any successful partnership, whether it's personal or professional.

When 1 + 1 + 1 = 5

Developing a vision for what you want is hard. Having the guts to pull the trigger and pursue it is harder. If you try to do either entirely on your own, success is almost impossible.

Consider the power of one plus one:

- Bill Hewlett and Dave Packard built HP.
- Coco Chanel and Pierre Wertheimer built Chanel Parfum.
- Bill Gates and Paul Allen built Microsoft.
- Steve Jobs and Steve Wozniak built Apple.
- Ben Cohen and Jerry Greenfield built Ben & Jerry's Ice Cream.
- Larry Page and Sergey Brin built Google.

Let's take a closer look at Steve Jobs and Steve Wozniak. Steve Jobs sucked at real engineering. He could conceive of wonderful product innovations, talk customers into buying and suppliers into providing credit, but he couldn't design the product. For that he needed a partner: Wozniak. Wozniak marveled at the way Jobs interacted with people. He was amazed when Jobs would come back with an order for something that didn't yet exist. He couldn't have done it. But he could certainly design the products that didn't exist (like a keyboard-to-display interface)—and he did it in a fraction of the time it took other designers to do it. Partnership. The whole was greater than the sum of its parts.

Most people who achieve prosperity (however you define it) find a way to separate themselves from the crowd, to do things differently than others have done them. It makes sense. If you approach a project, a business idea, or a market strategy the same way that most others do, why should you expect anything but average results? The same is true of the more personal aspects of your vision of prosperity: Making great strides requires doing things that can be difficult and therefore are things that most people are not willing to do. The problem with leaving the familiar behind and pursuing something difficult is that it can be lonely.

Having a partner on your side, and preferably more than one, can help you make all sorts of leaps and shortcuts to achieve what you want. The right partners will understand your world and help you develop your ideas. They might help you shortcut your professional growth. They might help you access opportunities faster because they know your strengths and believe in you. They can help get you onto your personal path to prosperity earlier in life. They encourage you to do things when you might naturally hold back—like pushing you to go for a promotion that you aren't sure you're ready for or pushing you to pursue something new in your personal life. They push you to do something. If you want to take the entrepreneurial path, the right partner or partners will help you think through the process of leaving the safety of an organization and starting your own. Partners can offset your weaknesses, bring more compelling ideas to the table, and make $1 + 1 + 1 = 5$.

More important, great partners make everything more fun. If you are doing it right, pursuing any vision should be fun. And an activity is ten times more fun when shared with people who understand what you're doing, are "all in" just like you, and care about you and your success.

Partners encourage you to be fearless, because being fearless is easier when you know you have a partner who will be there to support you if you crash and burn.

Expanding the Partnership Concept

Tommy Spaulding, author of *It's Not Just Who You Know* helped me understand that the partnership concept doesn't have to be limited to just a few people in your life. The first time I met Tommy, he kind of freaked me out. I've never talked to someone who was so laser focused on understanding who I was and how he could help me. He smiled, listened intently, and asked probing questions to make sure he understood my issues and how they overlapped with his life experience. Then, during that first meeting and across our next several interactions (which he initiated), he shared wisdom that, as a first-time author, I found to be invaluable. His expectation about what he would get in return? Not a thing.

In those interactions, I felt that he was my partner. No, not a lifelong, "I'll support you through anything" kind of partner, but absolutely a "I'm here to help you succeed because we're on similar paths, and maybe you'll be able to help me, too" kind of partner.

Tommy teaches the lesson of networking with people because you are genuinely more interested in "giving" than "getting." This shift in focus makes all the difference in developing a meaningful relationship that meets my definition of a partner. His book isn't just another book about networking; instead it's a book about net-*giving*. "Networking is all about *you*," he wrote. "Netgiving is all about *others*. Networking is all about collecting contacts and using those contacts for *personal* gain. Netgiving is all about building relationships that help *others* around you succeed. Networking is about winning friends and influencing people for personal gain. Netgiving is about influencing friends to make a difference."[10]

Even though throughout my life I have been fortunate enough to have many people work by my side and support my success, until I talked with Tommy, I believed that partners were a small number of people whom you cared deeply about and whom you could trust with your life. Tommy's message is, Why stop there? He has built a life full of partners who help each other pursue

10. Tommy Spaulding, *It's Not Just Who You Know* (New York: Crown Business, 2010), 147.

prosperity, and I can tell you from personal experience that he walks the talk. After four or five interactions, he started signing his e-mail, "Love, Tommy." I have a pretty well-developed bullshit detector, and Tommy registers a zero. He really means what he says and, even though he's not looking for it, I can't wait until I have a chance to help him with one of his challenges.

What Tommy exemplifies is the concept that for each iteration of the Prosperity Cycle, you may need or develop new partnerships. Yes, your long-term, friends-for-life partners will always be by your side, but for each endeavor, you need to get the right people on your bus, to co-opt a phrase from Jim Collins. Look for people who have shared goals, and explore how you can help each other. Expand your idea of partners beyond a few best friends or a couple of business partners or your spouse or life partner to a much broader group. Recruit allies wherever you go by genuinely caring about other people first and then elevating them to partners by identifying common interests and reciprocal netgiving.

How Do You Find Great Partners?

Even if you approach relationships the way Tommy does and develop a broad base of partners, you will find that a subset of these will rise to a higher level of importance in your life than others. Why? Partly because of the circumstances of your relationship, such as how frequently you interact, but also because of key factors that make some partners great. Take a look at the factors I've listed below as you think about the relationships that you have in your life that might rise to the level of great partnerships.

Characteristics of a Great Partner

- Someone who shares your values
- Someone who knows you well
- Someone who has your best interests at heart
- Someone whose opinion you value
- Someone who understands what you do
- Someone who is fun to be around
- Bonus: Someone who balances your strengths

Let's explore each point.

A conversation with someone who shares your core values starts at a much higher level. You get to skip the warm-up act and jump right into the main event. If you both agree on what's important and the right way to do things, you start the conversation by exploring how the issue at hand impacts those things. You spend more time figuring out how to move forward and less time rehashing fundamental disagreements.

Nothing is more powerful than the type of familiarity you get when you let your guard down and discover that you can trust somebody implicitly. This is what it means for a partner to know you well. We've all had this type of familiarity—with family and friends and occasionally with colleagues. It comes at different times in different relationships, sometimes after years of knowing somebody and sometimes after hours. A relationship like this is incredibly efficient because it is honest. No time is wasted sugarcoating. A partner who knows you well and whom you can trust will have no problem calling you out if you're taking a position that doesn't jibe with what he or she knows about you.

If you have any doubt whether a person has your best interests at heart, that person isn't your partner. Again, it all comes back to trust. You should be able to say anything to a person who supports you unconditionally—who has your back—without fear of judgment or retribution. And you should feel confident that anything this person says or does, even if you don't agree, is because he wants the best for you. This is true just as much in business partnerships as it is in personal. In a partnership based on the best interests of each party, personal filters are not necessary. The value of every interaction is increased, and the timeline from idea to action is reduced. This is a relationship that keeps no secrets.

Of course, you must value the opinion of your partner. This is a natural result of the points I've already made, but it also says something about the depth of knowledge and expertise that a person has developed in a particular arena, particularly if it is complementary to your own. Regardless of how original your ideas are, people are working in adjacent areas whose effort and learning represent work that you can skip if you can apply what they have already worked to understand. Those who qualify as great partners will gladly offer their sage advice, helping to advance your thinking by leveraging their own experiences. Through this synergistic process, they'll help you to move your plan ahead faster and in a more fruitful direction. Why would they do this? Because you have developed a relationship, they care about you, and they want to help you in any way they can. Additionally, they know that you would do the same for them (and probably have) as they pursue their own personal visions.

Life is too short to hang out with people you don't enjoy being around. A great partner (in business or in a relationship) is someone that you can spend hours with without tension and without boredom—and will undoubtedly share your sense of humor.

Finally, the bonus attribute is strengths that balance your own. Although not a necessity in every great partner, complementary strengths can be very important in some types of partnerships, particularly business partnerships or any partnership where you are sharing the responsibility as a team for moving a project forward. The work you began in shortcut 3 to understand your strengths will help you identify partners who can complement your efforts in reaching a goal.

This list might seem daunting. How many people can you think of in your life who qualify as great partners? I have hundreds of people that I call my friends and many whom I now consider to be partners, but I can count on one hand the number of great partners with whom I would be comfortable sharing a personal vision and plan to pursue it: none from high school, two from my five years of college, and four from my professional career (okay, I can count them on 1.2 hands).

I'm sure that you have partner potentials in your life that you aren't fully tapping—family members, friends, colleagues. But if you're expecting them to invest in a partnership with you—it is an investment of time and energy, and sometimes money if it's business—you have to invest in them first.

Getting Pragmatic About Partnerships

Organizational structure has come a long way over the course of my career. In the early days, it was dominated by a command-and-control mentality. If you were the boss, you called the shots and your subordinates hopped to it. Simple, yes, but spectacularly ineffective when compared with a more modern environment where a highly mobile workforce is attracted and motivated through the alignment of their talents and interests—where work is accomplished within a web of dotted lines and relationships that exist to serve the customer.

People capable of establishing productive partnerships based on trust thrive in this environment, while people basing their interaction style on a win–lose, trust-sucking, zero-sum mentality are left behind. As I explained in shortcut 7, enthusiastically adopting someone else's perspective and adding value to help advance his or her ideas is a great way to build trust. In shortcut 8 we extended this concept by talking about an even more powerful way to build the trust that fuels productive partnerships—by demonstrating that you genuinely care.

In order to establish a great partnership, you first must *be* a great partner. You have to offer everything that you expect to get from your partner: respect, trust, understanding, and genuine caring. Both parties need to know that by having each other's back and cooperatively leveraging their respective strengths, the sum of their achievements will be much greater than the sum of their individual abilities—that they will both benefit, even if that does not happen immediately.

Most of what I learned about successful partnering I learned from my experience at Peak Industries. Because we were a start-up and operating in the hypercompetitive field of contract manufacturing, I needed partners capable of producing a level of productivity that I had never seen before. I ended up finding four of them. I recruited one trusted colleague from Emerson Electric and watched the other three use the skills recommended in this book to emerge as the company's leaders. The five of us ended up creating a highly marketable medical device capability that, when combined with a winning company culture, formed the engine behind a company that was able to grow to employ over three hundred people and generate sales of over $70 million.

The company's constant growth left little time for less-than-critical activities, like developing the values that would guide our efforts and the strategic plans we used to coordinate the development of our continually evolving capabilities. In order to make time for these activities, we decided to hold our strategy sessions every other Thursday night after the production day ended. These biweekly sessions took our partnership to a new level. Each of us would keep track of the company issues that needed to be addressed and would come to the meeting with a list. Together we would prioritize the list and dive into issue after issue. We created an atmosphere of mutual respect where anyone could voice an opinion without being judged. We dealt with big issues while keeping the mood light and the jokes coming. We had each other's best interests at heart, we had shared values (written!), and we respected each partner's area of expertise (engineering, production, sales, finance). And above all, we enjoyed each other's company enough that spending fourteen hours together (the regular workday plus the evening strategy session) every other Thursday wasn't stressful; it was fun.

If you want partnerships like this, you have to put yourself out there and prove to those around you that you're up for the challenge.

———————————————————

A small number of people in the world are highly successful and don't seem to give a damn what anyone else thinks. They come up with a compelling vision and then charge headlong into the effort to make the vision a reality. They don't worry about failure, they ignore criticism, and they have no need for anyone else's buy-in. God bless America for creating men and women like these. Their efforts make our world a better place and make the United States the birthplace of the most innovative companies in the world. But they are a rare breed. For every one of them, thousands of people like me need help overcoming the gravitational pull of conventional thinking. Having someone whom you trust, who can objectively review your ideas, and who will encourage you to go for it—whatever "it" is—is incredibly powerful. Surround yourself with as many of those people as possible, in every endeavor.

Finding the Shortcut

- Perhaps the biggest benefit of having a trusted business or life partner is to help you make the really big decisions—the decisions that will make a dramatic difference in your life but could also have a significant downside. What are the big ideas rolling around in your head that you have not shared with anyone else? Imagine how much progress you could make if you had people in your life who could help to shape these ideas or even pull the trigger on one.
- Regardless of the other leadership traits you currently possess, adopting a carefrontation mindset within existing relationships will take you to another level. Think about the people around you who believe in you and are demonstrating a limiting behavior that you can help them understand.

Do Something

- Read Tommy Spaulding's *It's Not Just Who You Know* to internalize the behaviors that will guarantee an abundance of great partner candidates.

- Take a single goal that is part of your vision and identify potential partners to help you achieve that goal. Make a list of people already in your life that have the characteristics of a great partner. Rate them from 1 to 5 for each of the partner attributes listed on page 177, and total the scores for an indication of your strongest partner candidates.

- If you struck out in identifying potential partners who are already in your life, identify friends and business associates whom you respect and who you believe could make great partners and start designing ways to spend more time with them. Remember, this will probably start by giving them support first.

SHORTCUT 10: Find a Mentor, or Three

Geo Concepcion grew up in a rough, low-income neighborhood on the north side of Chicago. Even though he never got to know his father and money was always tight, Geo thinks he was pretty lucky. His mom had a great set of values that included a belief that nothing was more important than education. She even moved Geo into the best public school she could find when his first grade teacher told her that Geo wasn't being challenged.

But it wasn't until Geo reached middle school that he began to understand the hardships of the world he lived in and to sense his own primal cues. He wanted to get out from under the burden of poverty. Life at this age revolved around baseball for Geo, but his family couldn't afford to replace his worn-out mitt. More humiliating were the times when Geo had to impose on his friends to ask for help meeting basic daily needs. Having decided that he was going to create a better life for himself, and with help from his mom, Geo launched his Prosperity Cycle by deciding to earn the grades in middle school that would put him on the path toward the Whitney Young Magnet High School, one of the best public college preparatory high schools in the area.

And that's when things got interesting.

After a year or so in his new high school, Geo resolved to learn more about finance and signed up for his high school's accounting class. As part of the accounting class, a Junior Achievement volunteer, Geoff Smart, came in and taught a ten-week class on entrepreneurship. You may have heard of Geoff. He's the bestselling author of *Who* and *Leadocracy*, and CEO of ghSMART, a leadership consulting company. In a classroom full of students, Geoff couldn't help but notice Geo. His enthusiasm for the course was over the top. Geo was fascinated by the lectures and would hang out after class and talk to Geoff about potential careers. Geo said he "would pepper Geoff with questions and probably was quite a nuisance." From Geoff's perspective, Geo came off as enthusiastic, knowledgeable, and intelligent. In Geo's words, "Geoff gave me the resources to think about a much more demanding career path than I would have pursued otherwise."

This would be the start of a powerful mentoring relationship for Geo.

By the end of the ten-week course, Geo had let Geoff know about his goal to someday work on Wall Street. In return, Geoff offered Geo his contact information and invited him to keep in touch periodically if he wanted to. As Geoff described it, "I wasn't going to chase this kid, but if he wanted to take the initiative to call me, I've always got time to let a student pick my brain. It was very much up to him. And to his credit he has followed up ever since."

A mentor can offer you many things, but a critical component is that he will break news that you might not want to hear. When Geo shared his goal of going to work for a leading Wall Street firm, Geoff told him that he needed to aim for a 4.0 in college. Geo had been more of a B student in high school yet still leveraged his hard work and ambition into a full-ride scholarship to DePaul University. When Geoff delivered his dose of reality, Geo demonstrated his commitment by taking his effort to a new level, earning a 3.97 by the time he graduated from DePaul.

Again, Geo found that his effort paid off. Geoff called it one of the proudest days of his life when Geo called him to say that he had earned not one but four offers from top-tier financial firms. Geo had just achieved the goal that had motivated him for the last six years.

Geoff finds it incredibly satisfying, in a mentoring relationship or otherwise, "to work with someone who acts on my counsel and achieves more because of it." And with Geo in particular, he found his chats were fun, useful, and low hassle—because Geo made them that way. Geo understood that Geoff was a very busy guy and made sure he didn't waste his time. He checked in only a few times a year and only when he needed insight on a big decision or opportunity.

Today, Geo Concepcion is a trader for a financial firm that manages over $6.5 billion in investments. At age twenty-five he is just now becoming conscious of how and when he entered the Prosperity Cycle. Until recently, his journey from disadvantaged kid to trader seemed to him like a series of lucky or random events that culminated in his current job. But now that he is involved in coaching other young people, he's realizing that his path wasn't random at all. But it was always clear to him how important mentoring was to his success. "I look at the people that I get to work with and the different experience that I've had and it's very, very cool. Without Geoff's mentorship, there's no way I would have achieved my goal of working for a top Wall Street firm, much less landed my current job."

Why You Need a Mentor

There's working hard and there's working smart. Working smart requires you to learn from the best, but mentoring takes that idea a step further. Instead of learning from people who are a bit more knowledgeable than you or may be on the same path, mentoring offers you an opportunity to learn from someone who has successfully achieved what you want to achieve and has the experience and wisdom to offer sound, valid, and possibly life-changing guidance and opportunities.

The mountain that you are about to climb can look intimidating from the bottom. Getting advice from someone who has climbed it before can give you the confidence that it can be done, that you can do it. Whether your vision is to become a leader within a large corporation or the chief executive of your own start-up, one of the toughest hurdles you will face is the need to believe you can actually do it. Most of us sell ourselves short and don't aim high enough. An experienced mentor can take the pie-in-the-sky vision that you are hesitant to even say out loud and, through experience and personal example, lead you to the point where you can see yourself making it happen.

But a mentor can offer much more than inspiration: A mentor can open your eyes to possibilities that you didn't even know existed—opportunities that might fit your desires and abilities better than anything you had considered. A mentor can put the right tool in your hand at the right time. The right mentor can allow you to take action—the right action—before you run out of time, money, energy, or inspiration or before somebody else beats you to the punch. A mentor can open doors for you that would be difficult, if not impossible, for you to open yourself. People are out there just waiting to employ you, invest in you, promote you, and believe in you. They just don't know it yet. The right mentor can help.

More than giving you advice on how to solve an immediate problem, a mentor can advise you on what prosperity even means to you. Before you set off for a distant destination, it pays to think through whether you really want to go there. It's never too early to work with a mentor—even while you are sorting out your personal vision. Taking the wrong path can delay your journey to prosperity interminably. A mentor can keep you from going down any number of dead ends and keep you on the shortest path to prosperity.

A mentor is a great person to turn to when you face a decision that has fundamental implications for the prosperous life you envision. For smaller decisions that are issue specific and require someone with a particular experience or knowledge base, you might turn instead to a more readily available resource—someone who may not know you as well but has the experience to provide valuable guidance for the issue at hand.

In America, historically there has been a focus on self-reliance, and that's not a bad thing. Ultimately, it is up to each of us to make things happen in our lives. But we shouldn't get caught up in a mindset that says we always have to do everything on our own. We don't. It's okay to ask for help.

Sometimes a Guide Is All You Need

Geoff isn't the only mentor that Geo has had. Before Geoff, Geo looked to a baseball coach and a teacher for guidance, and after landing his first job in finance, Geo looked to a small number of more experienced colleagues to guide him. In fact, *guide* may be a better word than *mentor* for people who can provide you with direction within a narrowly defined field or for a brief period of time.

It is no secret that as the world has gotten more complex, the professionals who thrive within it have gotten more specialized. A generation ago, a mentor for a young person in banking could have provided advice on almost any subject that came up. Today, if a similar young person is trying to figure out which potential employer's hedge fund strategy is a better fit for his strengths, he had better have an adviser who understands the subtle differences. A guide is someone who has the experience you need to make the right decision and doesn't necessarily need to know you as well as a mentor in order to add value. By engaging the expert, you can save precious time with your mentor for big-picture questions while getting better advice from someone who finds it easy to provide it.

More guide candidates are available to you than there are mentors, those who have taken the time to understand you and your unique path to prosperity. The power of social networking is that you can build a network of potential guides, people you may need to turn to when you hit a road block for a bit of very targeted advice. Utilizing a guide relationship opens up more resources to you and is more likely to be a netgiving opportunity—a chance for a two-way exchange of help. That said, the difference between a guide and a mentor is subtle. More often a guide is somebody who is not a peer, who isn't on the path alongside you but who has been where you need to go and can help you understand the twists and turns in the path directly ahead of you.

What Makes a Good Mentor?

Whether you are in high school or are a mid-career professional, you should be looking for the same fundamentals in your mentoring relationships. The best are marked by a respectful, curious, and self-starting mentee and a mentor who is experienced and successful, has a win–win personality, and enjoys enabling the success of someone traveling a similar career path.

Most effective mentorships occur between two people who have invested time in the process of coming to know, respect, and care about each other. Why? It's difficult to be a good mentor to someone you haven't taken the time to get to know. You have to care enough to dedicate precious time to mentoring activities, and that won't happen until you have come to know and respect your mentee. From the mentee's perspective, it takes time before you feel comfortable entrusting your hopes and dreams to someone you haven't already come to know and respect. That's why the most natural mentorships aren't arranged marriages but are relationships that begin as something else and evolve into a mentorship over time.

Prime candidates for mentors are current or former bosses, teachers, or family friends. Mentorships like these are extremely powerful. Mentors have the opportunity to combine their personal relationships with a mentee with a core competence in their area of interest. They build on an existing foundation of mutual respect and, from there, forge ahead into the fun stuff—the discussion of what the mentee wants to achieve and the shortest path to realizing it, based on the mentor's experience.

If you are fortunate enough to know someone like this, you're already a step ahead. It's more likely, however, that you don't have a close relationship with somebody who has already achieved many of the things you would like to achieve. So you have to go find a mentor with a proven track record of success who is willing to take the time to understand your aspirations and, through expert guidance, increase your odds of achieving them.

To help you assess mentor candidates, use the attributes shown here.

Attributes of a Great Mentor

Someone who:

- Has achieved success and has deep experience in your area of focus.
- Cares about you and your development. This interest could be motivated by a familial bond, friendship, professional relationship, or simply the great feeling generated by helping another person succeed.
- Is accessible. Meetings don't need to be face-to-face. The deeper the relationship, the more possible it is to tackle tough subjects on the phone, Skype, or over e-mail.
- Listens well. Think twice before choosing a mentor who enjoys hearing himself talk more than understanding your perspective.
- Gives advice, not directives. A good mentor is there to leverage his or her experience and contacts to help you achieve your goals, not to tell you what to do.
- Has demonstrated the high level of confidentiality essential to frank discussions and personal exploration.
- Exhibits traits that you would like to emulate. Whether your mentor is ethical and gracious or shady and pompous, over time you will begin to emulate that behavior.

As you think about potential mentors in your life, assess their relative strengths and weaknesses. Some will have more experience in your area of interest, while others may offer a better personal connection. Refer to the exercises at the end of this shortcut to help you consider candidates.

I've been lucky enough to have a number of important mentors in my life. The most important was my father. I could confide anything to him without fear of being judged or looking foolish; having the confidence to ask "dumb" questions is key. He had experience with businesses of all shapes and sizes, and he was a numbers guy. He grilled me for business plans and financial projections, and those projections killed a lot of ideas that sounded pretty good in my head but would have led me down a disastrous path. I had no doubt that he had my best interests at heart. While he wasn't an entrepreneur, he believed that it was the surest path to the prosperity I wanted. And he told me the single most valuable piece of advice that anyone has ever given me: It didn't matter much where I started my entrepreneurial journey. He was confident that over time I would be able to direct my path toward what I wanted. The important part was to get in the game. He gave me the confidence to pull the trigger.

But I developed another mentoring relationship through pure chutzpah. When I knew that I wanted to explore an entrepreneurial path, I started talking to anyone I knew who I thought could tell me about starting or operating a small company. The problem was that I didn't know that many people with relevant experience. So I would chat up anyone I came into contact with about the subject, including complete strangers. One evening I was returning to Denver from a business trip and found myself sitting with the only other passenger on an airport shuttle bus. Small talk led us to discover that we both lived in Fort Collins and that my fellow traveler, Fred Gardner, was the president of a commercial sign company, Gardner Signs. In the ten minutes or so we had together, I managed to convey an interest in his company and a desire to learn more about his story. We exchanged business cards. I'm sure he thought he'd never hear from me again.

He was wrong. Within a week I followed up with a phone call, and after another pleasant conversation, I asked if he and his wife would like to join my wife and me for dinner at our home. In retrospect, I can't believe I did that. Neither could his wife, Denise. She later admitted that she was sure that they were in for an evening of Amway sales; I think they had a side bet on it. In any case, we had a great evening. I learned a ton from Fred's story of becoming the president of his own company. In subsequent conversations, Fred educated me on the good and the bad of small business ownership and was the first one to recommend an organization called Young Presidents' Organization (YPO), an organization that ended up being a lifesaver by supplying a global pool of peers who were doing what I was doing and could suggest solutions to the myriad problems that I would encounter over the next ten years.

Twenty years later, Fred and Denise are still our dear friends. And I would not have known him if I had not been willing to get out of my comfort zone and chat up a stranger. Just as you are surrounded by great business opportunities, you are also surrounded by incredible resources on a daily basis. Think about this the next time you are getting coffee, working out, sitting on an airplane, or eating alone. In fact, take Keith Ferrazzi's advice and *Never Eat Alone*.

Earn the Right to Be Mentored

A cautionary note: A great mentor is not a crutch, will not do your work for you, and won't turn you on to an opportunity that you don't deserve. Advice from a mentor can be invaluable, and all that most mentors want in return is a word of thanks and the ability to take pride in an accomplishment that their experience helped support. But, like almost every other recommendation in this book, getting the full benefit of a mentorship is a lot of work.

The world we live in is a complex place, and when you finally figure out how a piece of it works, you want to shout it out loud. That is how a mentor thinks. It's even better when a hard-working young person shows an interest in hearing you explain it—especially if the listener goes on to leverage your advice into a remarkable achievement and you can say you helped him or her do it. So, if you have any doubts about your willingness to follow the advice of a mentor or in your ability or motivation to do the work required, please do the mentors of the world a big favor and don't approach them in the first place. They may put their reputations on the line by recommending you or offering you an opportunity. You had better be ready to deliver.

If you are able to find the right mentor and commit yourself to acting on his or her advice, don't forget to say thank you. It's the primary compensation the mentor is looking for. The best way to do this is by repeating the advice that a mentor gave you, showing how you put it to work, and sharing the great results you achieved because of it.

And when you do achieve the prosperity you've been striving for, pay it forward and become a mentor to somebody who has a lot to learn from you.

Finding the Shortcut

- Long-term relationships yield the most productive guides. Think about friends, family, and colleagues who have an interesting experience or background that you have not yet had the opportunity to explore. Next, expand your thinking to groups that are organized to bring people together in your area of interest. Research existing user groups, technical associations, and conferences.

- You would be surprised at the incredible resources that you come in contact with randomly or as a normal course of business. Challenge yourself to get out of your comfort zone and talk more with those around you, ask questions, and learn about them and their backgrounds. Connect with them on LinkedIn or another social network.

- All organizations need volunteers to advance the group's mission. What organizations could you help with research, outreach, or organization in order to forge valuable relationships?

Do Something

- Start networking with a purpose. Adding huge numbers to your LinkedIn Network has value, but not nearly as much as creating groups of a smaller number of high-value contacts where you can note the specific skills, experience, or connections that you may want to access later. In LinkedIn, you can use tags to group contacts in a variety of ways and then quickly access them when you need them.

- Brainstorm a list of family, friends, colleagues, bosses, former professors, and business leaders that you have come to know. Rate each on a scale of 1 to 5 for each of the following:
  - Level of success in their profession
  - Alignment of their profession with your passion

- How closely their values align with yours
- Your estimate of their interest in helping you or some-one like you
- Sort your list by the sum of the scores to give you a prioritized list of guides for your journey. When you face a new challenge, go here first.
- Whenever you approach a contact or someone on your list for help, use an approach that shows respect, gratitude, and a desire to support their initiatives if it is within your ability to do so.

I BELIEVE IN YOU

I know quite certainly that I myself have no special talent; curiosity, obsession and dogged endurance, combined with self-criticism, have brought me to my ideas.

—Albert Einstein

Don't think you can draw parallels between Albert Einstein and yourself? Think again. When you achieve prosperity you are going to feel the same way that Einstein did—that you aren't particularly gifted, but rather your dogged pursuit of and thousands of hours invested in your passion led you to a level of knowledge and insight that made you seem gifted to others. You will understand that prosperity is the way that one is repaid for inspired effort—an effort that isn't hard to generate when it is motivated by a personal passion and reinforced by successive achievements.

At this point, having read this book (many thanks!), you have a choice to make. You can either make the commitment to enter your own Prosperity Cycle and see where it takes you, or take the path of least resistance to your future life. For many of you, the path of least resistance means following the example of parents, advisers, peers, or other influential people in your life and traveling a path that has become familiar to you. You may not have any definitive ideas about your passions and are simply putting one foot in front of the other. If so, you owe it to yourself to invest some time to explore your path to prosperity. Use this book as a way to figure out what makes work seem like play. If it is not what you are currently doing, make a change and find a way to rapidly gain a differentiating level of knowledge, confidence, and insight within your true passion. And while you are getting down your learning curve, make sure you find the time to identify the people who will help you achieve your personal vision of prosperity.

David, Shannon, Amber, Steve, Ernest, Mike, Craig, Geo, and Ken beat the odds and independently figured out what a prosperous life meant to them, but it wasn't easy, and they all wish that someone had helped them understand the transformative process they were experiencing. So they shared their stories with me in the hope that it would make the process easier for others. I hope I was able to convey a small portion of the passion that was so clearly evident to me when I listened to them talk about the meaningful lives that they have built for themselves.

So go make something happen! And do it while you are young. You have less to lose and more of the most critical ingredients to give—time, energy, and a sense that anything is possible, which of course, it is. Nothing in your background, upbringing, financial resources, or lack of personal connections can get in the way. Please don't let this book leave your backpack, briefcase, or reader before you map your shortcut to prosperity and take the first step onto it. And don't forget to check in at www.shortcut-toprosperity.com for new ideas and to see how others are faring with their own pursuits.

Perhaps the last thing I can offer you is something that is as simple as it is valuable—a declaration that *I believe in you*. When I was in the middle of this book project, my friend and best-selling author Tommy Spaulding told me that he believed in the *Shortcut to Prosperity*, and he believed in me. When he said it, we hadn't known each other long, and he was basing his comments on nothing more than a chapter outline and my maniacal enthusiasm for the project. He knew that's all I needed. So let me return the favor by telling you with the utmost sincerity that I believe in you. I believe in your ability to develop an inspiring personal vision and, as Steve Jobs once said, to put your own dent in the universe by making that vision a reality.

Have fun, and use the website to let me know how it's going.

ACKNOWLEDGMENTS

As our daughters, Kate and Maren, left Colorado to study in Connecticut, I found myself wondering how I could help them take a shorter path to the incredibly fulfilling life that took Jenny and me twenty-five years of trial and error to achieve. As I thought about how to share what we have learned, I realized that even though it was the right time for me to write a book, the girls were not yet ready to read it. *Shortcut to Prosperity* became the perfect vehicle to capture insight that I hope others will benefit from while creating an archive for the girls to draw on later. Kat and MZ, thanks for inspiring me to write this book and for the unexpected smile I have to explain to colleagues every time they catch me pondering your latest escapades.

Clint Greenleaf, this book would not have existed had I not read about you in *Forbes* magazine. Seeing you barefoot, smiling, and surrounded by piles of Greenleaf books made me believe that you just might get what I was trying to do. Lari Bishop, my editor and coach, many thanks for your patience in waiting for my true voice to finally appear and for shaping my thoughts into a book with the perfect tone and feel—the one that I could never have discovered without your firm hand on the tiller. To the rest of the team at Greenleaf—Sheila Parr in design, Chris McRay in production, Abby Kitten in marketing—thank you for guiding this project onward.

To my friends at Peak Industries, the essence of this book comes directly from what we learned together during the nine years we spent creating the coolest organization that I will ever have the privilege to be part of. Your commitment to excellence, to our customers, and to each other continues to inspire me to this day. I love you all.

Thank you, Amber, Craig, David, Ernest, Geo, Ken, Mike, Mike, Shannon, and Steve. Your stories are as inspirational as they are instructive, bringing to life the concepts that I hope will change lives. Special thanks to all of you who helped shape the book content by sharing your perspectives with me, especially Justin Brandon, Jason Christie, Pam Hatcher, and Rich Hoops. Reviewing my notes from our conversations was often helpful in distilling a key point to its essence. And a tip of the hat to my friends Ted Harris, Rick Green, Geoff Smart, and the great people at Junior Achievement for helping me find these incredible people.

Writing this book was much lonelier and harder than I had imagined. I could never have completed the journey without the monthly pep talks that I received from my YPO forum members Matt Autterson, Mark Honnen, Mark Kalkus, Rich Kylberg, Mike Long, Jimmy Miller, and Bruce Porter. I would do anything for you guys.

Most importantly, what can I say to the people who instilled in me the passion to explore, endeavor, savor, and share all that our wonderful world has to offer? Tom, Jeanette, Eric, and Jennifer Hopkins, you are the best family a boy could have and I don't tell any of you that often enough. I am truly blessed.

RESOURCES

As you make progress on your own journey to prosperity please check in with me at

www.shortcuttoprosperity.com

and let me know what you are learning and to find resources and information to help you along your path. The website was designed to allow us to continue our dialog, but more importantly, to allow you to share your experiences with others and learn more along the way.

I would also recommend that you research three organizations that have helped many other people achieve prosperity.

- **Junior Achievement** (www.ja.org): Junior Achievement is a well-run organization that brings experienced business people into the classroom to teach nontraditional subjects related to entrepreneurship and financial literacy. For those of you fortunate enough and enterprising enough to be reading this while still in high school, I highly recommend you find the

Junior Achievement office that is closest to you and contact them. For those of you well into your careers and ready to share your knowledge with hungry minds, contact Junior Achievement for mentoring and teaching opportunities.

- **Entrepreneurs' Organization** (www.eonetwork.org): If you have chosen an entrepreneur's path and have founded or are running an organization that is capable of generating annual sales of at least $1 million, this is a great organization for you. EO, with more than eight thousand members, combines peer-to-peer exchange with targeted education at the local and international levels to help entrepreneurs and the organizations they lead.
- **Young President's Organization** (www.ypo.org): For leaders who are younger than 45 years of age and leading companies with revenues over $8 million, please don't pass up the opportunity to experience YPO. The organization's mission is to improve the leadership of its members through education and idea exchange. Every one of its over twelve thousand members will tell you that YPO has been instrumental in their ability to deal with the business and personal issues that come with leading a larger organization.

INDEX

ABOUT THE AUTHOR

Mark Hopkins earned engineering degrees from Cornell and Stanford and then spent the next twenty-five years deciphering the factors that make some people prosperous, successful, and happy. In 1996, after building a leadership career with companies like Hewlett-Packard and Emerson Electric, Mark founded Peak Industries, a medical device contract manufacturer, which he grew to $75 million and later sold to Delphi. He then founded Crescendo Capital Partners, a private equity firm, and Catalyst, a private foundation supporting Colorado-based nonprofits and microlending in the developing world. He is a member of the Chief Executives Organization, a partner in Social Venture Partners' Boulder chapter, and on the board of governors for Opportunity International. He has led YPO Global Leadership Workshops around the world.